BEGINNER**BLUES** GUITAR**SOLOING**

The Complete Guide to Mastering the Language & Techniques of Blues Guitar

JOSEPH**ALEXANDER**

FUNDAMENTAL**CHANGES**

Beginner Blues Guitar Soloing

The Complete Guide to Mastering the Language & Techniques of Blues Guitar

ISBN: 978-1-78933-147-9

Published by **www.fundamental-changes.com**

Copyright © 2019 Joseph Alexander

Edited by Tim Pettingale

The moral right of this author has been asserted.

www.fundamental-changes.com

Twitter: @guitar_joseph

Over 10,000 fans on Facebook: **FundamentalChangesInGuitar**

Instagram: **FundamentalChanges**

For over 350 Free Guitar Lessons with Videos Check Out

www.fundamental-changes.com

Contents

Who is This Book For?

Hi, and welcome to the most complete course for guitarists who want to learn blues guitar soloing. This book is written as a guide for players who have been playing a while and have got to grips with the basics, like open chords, barre chords, picking single notes and strumming in time.

This book *won't* teach you to play guitar from scratch. For that, check out our range of beginner titles at:

https://www.fundamental-changes.com/product-category/guitar/beginner/

But if you can play guitar a little, and the blues is a form of music you want to explore, you're in the right place.

Blues soloing is one of the most expressive forms of improvisation for guitar and has a history that goes back over 100 years on the instrument. Its melodies and rhythms go back much further and its roots can be traced to African vocal music.

The blues is the backbone of most popular music, including jazz and rock. Once you have discovered blues guitar soloing, you'll quickly find that you can turn your hand to many different styles of music. This book will teach you how to play meaningful blues guitar solos from the ground up, with the minimum of theory. (I promise I'll only include it where absolutely necessary!)

What's to come...

In *Beginner Blues Guitar Soloing*, we'll start by taking a look at the *form* (structure) of the 12-bar Blues and learn how the music works as a foundation for beginning to solo. You'll learn the chord sequence and some great riffs you can use to jam with other people and play almost every blues song ever written. Once you've mastered the lessons here, you'll be able to play literally hundreds of blues guitar tunes by everyone from Muddy Waters to B.B. King to Jimi Hendrix.

When the basic structure is nailed, we'll move on to discover the main soloing sounds of the blues and the simple sequence notes that has underpinned the blues for over 100 years. This isn't a book of scales though – you'll immediately learn to use these notes to create meaningful phrases and licks that you can instantly use in your playing.

Next, we'll discover the essential art of *bending notes* – the most expressive and soulful tool in our arsenal as guitarists. You'll be amazed at how adding some simple bends to your phrases can turn a run of the mill sequence of notes into a classic blues guitar phrase that will move your audience. String bends are fundamental to playing the blues and it's important to introduce them into your playing as quickly as possible.

When you're bending like a pro, we'll go a bit deeper and discover how the real secret of great blues soloing isn't the notes that you play, but *when you play them*. I'll teach you one concept that I've taught literally thousands of students that will help you to move away from playing pre-rehearsed guitar licks and build your own, personal language of the blues. Blues licks are a very important part of soloing and this book contains hundreds of them, but learning the bluesy language of your heroes while developing your own style will make you a powerful player much more quickly.

From there, we will look at many other integral parts of soloing with the blues language:

We'll discuss dynamics (the articulation of your licks) and I'll teach you how, along with rhythm and pitch, there's a whole third dimension to playing the guitar that many players never discover. When you begin to combine *legato* ideas (hammer-ons and pull-offs) with picked notes, and learn to pick harder and softer, you'll be on your way to becoming a *storyteller* on your instrument – someone who can add subtle nuances to make the music come alive. We'll also discover the concept of *question and answer* or "call and response" phrasing to help you structure your solos and keep your audience engaged.

In the blues, there are many "set piece" licks that can be played at a specific point in the 12-bar sequence. These licks are called *turnarounds* (they literally help to "turn the music around" to the beginning so it can repeat for another loop). Great players know many of these turnarounds in different keys and I'll share some of my favourites here.

Finally, we'll round off by teaching you a couple of complete blues solos. You can practise these by playing along to the included backing tracks (which you can also use to jam along to). It's always important to have something to play and examples of how the techniques and licks in this book can combine together to create meaningful music.

Throughout, I'll teach you how to play in two of the main blues guitar keys and help you to spread your playing out all over the fretboard. Many players get stuck in just one position and this quickly leads to creative stagnation.

By the end of the book you'll be able to *improvise* (make up on the spot) 12-bar blues guitar solos and you'll sound like an authentic blues guitar player. However, the key to your progress will always be your ears. Listen to as much blues guitar music as you can and pay particular attention to the guitarists you love. A suggested listening list is included at the end of this book.

I can only show you so much here. If you're going to become a great player, you need to do a lot of homework. When you hear a blues lick that you like, stop the track you're listening to and try to work it out by ear. That's how every great guitarist learned to play the blues and transcribing their playing will help you to quickly develop a blues language that resonates with your soul and helps you to become a part of the long line of blues guitar tradition.

Please go and download the audio examples for this book now. Blues licks are extremely nuanced and there are some things that can't be perfectly expressed in notation/TAB. Listen carefully and use your ears!

Above all, have fun and keep your ears open.

Joseph

Get the Audio

The audio files for this book are available to download for free from **www.fundamental-changes.com.** The link is in the top right-hand corner. Simply select this book title from the drop-down menu and follow the instructions to get the audio.

We recommend that you download the files directly to your computer, not to your tablet, and extract them there before adding them to your media library. You can then put them on your tablet, iPod or burn them to CD. On the download page there is a help PDF and we also provide technical support via the contact form.

For over 350 Free Guitar Lessons with Videos Check out:

www.fundamental-changes.com

Over 10,000 fans on Facebook: **FundamentalChangesInGuitar**

Tag us for a share on Instagram: **FundamentalChanges**

Chapter One – The 12-Bar Blues

The backbone of the blues is the 12-bar chord sequence shown below. It forms the basis for everything you'll learn in this book, so you need to know its form and chords changes before you begin to solo.

Example 1a is a *lead sheet* that shows the basic structure of the 12-bar blues. There are no specific rhythm parts written or any indication of what scales to use for soloing. It is simply a road map of the chord sequence and shows which chords you should play and how long you need to play them for.

The four slash marks in each in *bar* (known as a *measure*) show that you play the notated chord for four (1/4 note) beats in each bar. Think of this as a road map that tells you (and the whole band) where the chords are going. How you play those chords is up to you, but they must all last for the notated duration otherwise the band will get lost.

This 12-bar blues is written in the key of A and consists of just three chords: A7, D7 and E7.

The first chord of A7 is played for four measures, then D7 is played for two measures before returning to A7 again for two measures. In the final line, the *turnaround* section begins and the chords of E7, D7, A7 and E7 are played for one measure each. I don't play the chords strictly as written on the audio track. The lead sheet is a guide to the chord lengths, not how to play them.

Example 1a

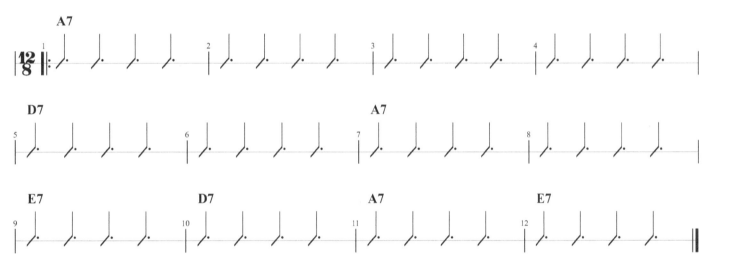

Let's begin with two simple strumming patterns you can use to play the 12-bar blues. Listen carefully to the audio tracks to get the correct feel and rhythm. There are many ways to play a rhythm guitar part in a blues, but the ones shown here will be a good start.

Example 1b uses common open chord shapes for all three dominant 7th chords. In a moment, we'll look at their barre chord equivalents, but this is a good place to start. Strum each chord shape with a downstroke of the pick and let all the notes ring for the full duration of the bar.

Count the four beats in each bar out loud to help you follow the chord durations. Keep repeating this and soon you will commit the entire sequence to memory. Play along with the blues backing track in A once you've memorised the chord sequence.

Example 1b

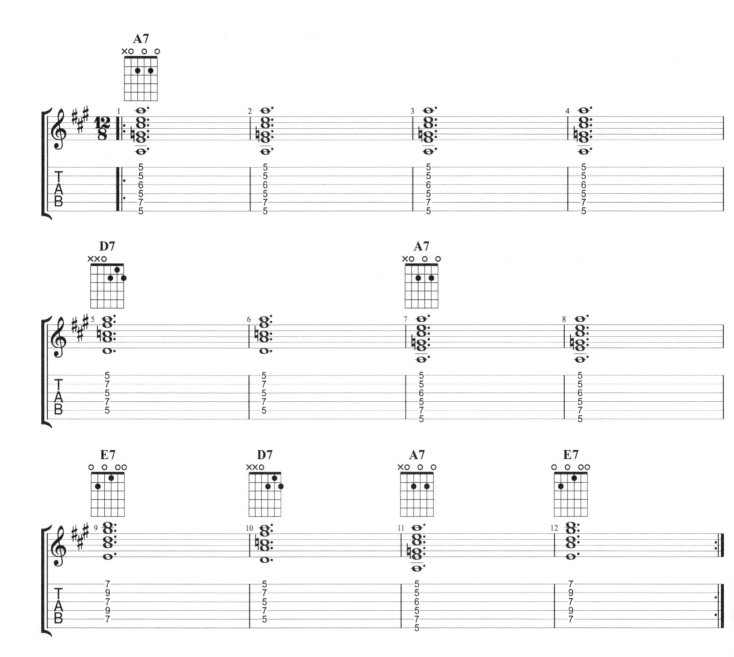

Now let's look at the barre chord versions of these chords. The beauty of the blues is, it's only three chords, so you'll never be overwhelmed with information! Below are chord diagrams for each of the three chords. The black squares show where the root note of each chord is located.

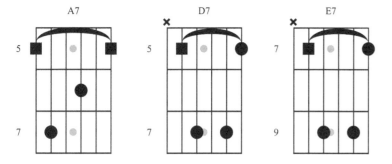

To play these chords, bar your index finger across the strings and press down firmly, then add the other fingers. To play A7, you'll bar across all six strings. To play the D7 and E7 chords, you'll only bar five strings – the low E string is not played (indicated by the small x above the string).

If you're not used to playing barre chords, it can take a while before you develop the fretting hand strength to hold down the chord and play it without any buzzes or squeaks. This is normal and just a matter of building muscle memory. Play through each chord in turn until you can sound all the notes clearly. Notice that the E7 chord is simply the D7 chord shape moved up two frets.

When you're comfortable with these chords, play through Example 1c. This example shows another important blues rhythm you should know. Here you will strum only on the 2nd and 4th beat of each bar to copy the *backbeat* of the drummer. Make the chords short (often called a "stab"). Beats 1 and 3 should be silent.

Example 1c

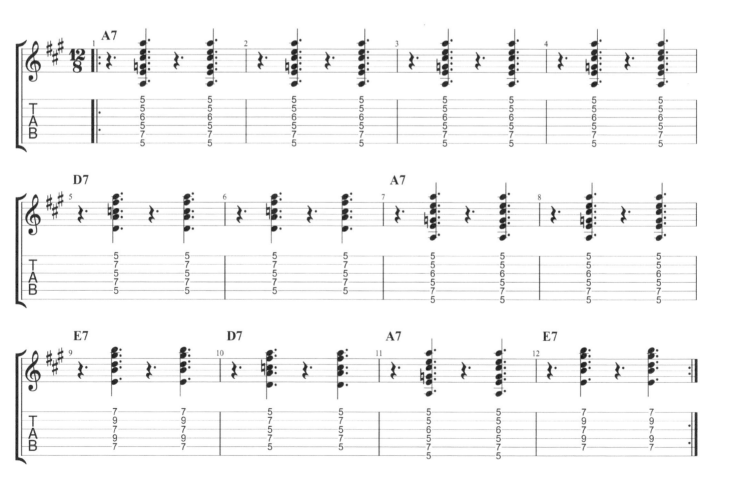

While the two previous examples help you to understand the structure of the 12-bar blues, they're a bit boring! Blues rhythm guitar is much more intricate and sophisticated than this. I'm going to show you a few ways to make this chord sequence a bit more interesting by using some classic riffs (but this isn't a book about rhythm guitar, it's a book about blues soloing so I don't have space to go into too much detail).

Rhythm guitar is fundamental to your ability to play the blues, so I strongly recommend you spend time studying it. My book *The Complete Guide to Blues Rhythm Guitar* covers this subject in great detail.

To make our chord sequence more interesting, let's move away from "big" chords and play some chord-based blues riffs. A riff is a small, repeated phrase on guitar. Riffs bridge the gap between chords and soloing.

Rhythm guitar isn't always about playing five- or six-string chords and many blues musicians use simple riffs and single- or double-note patterns to play amazing grooves. These come in especially handy when playing with other guitarists or keyboard players who are playing bigger chords.

Example 1d is a popular blues riff that combines open strings with a single-note melody. The rhythm is played in steady1/8th notes. Listen to the drums and stay in time with the track. Keep the open strings clean and use your first and third fingers to play the fretted notes.

Example 1d

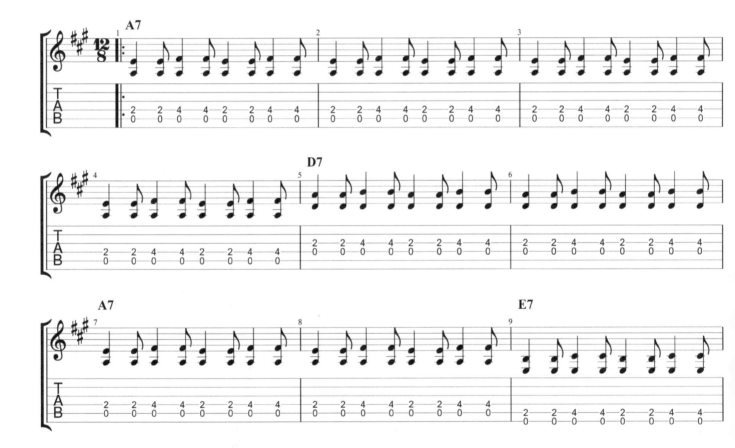

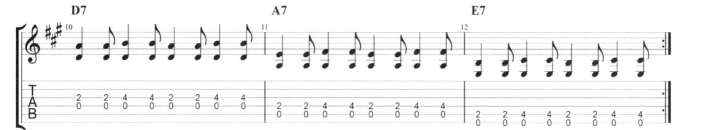

Now add your little finger on the 5th fret to enhance the riff a little.

Example 1e

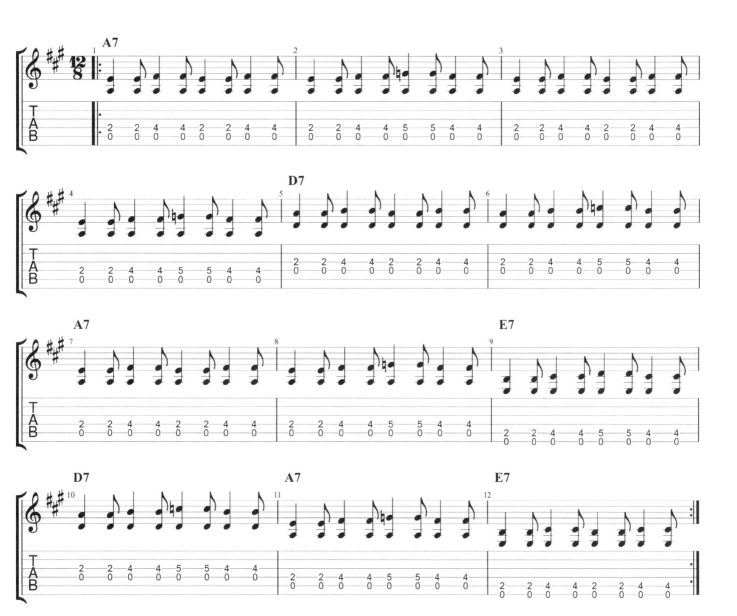

Let's add a little fill to this riff to make it a bit more interesting. Play the note on the 3rd fret with your second finger.

Example 1f

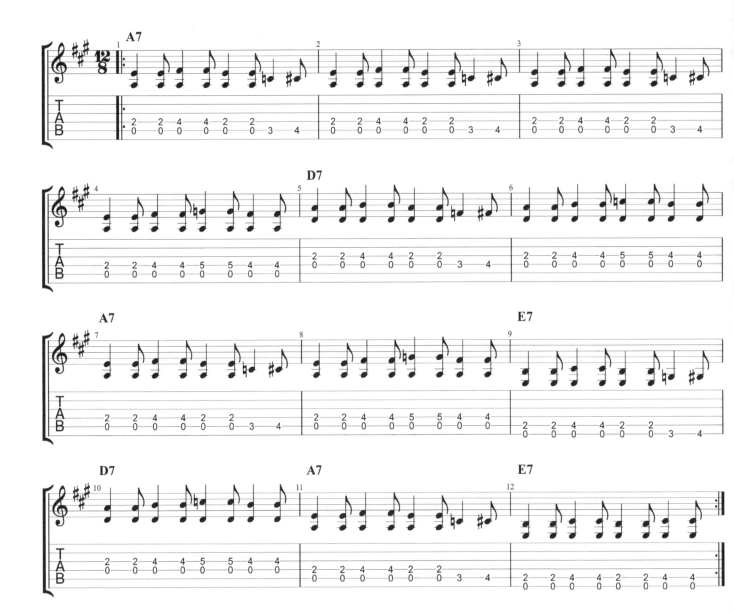

Here's a different kind of riff that's very common in blues. You'll have heard it on countless recordings, as it's one of the easiest but most effective ways of *spelling out* the chord changes. It's an effective alternative to playing chords and creates a "lead guitar" rhythm part in the style of Eric Clapton.

Example 1g

The previous examples were all in the key of A. Another common and important blues key is E. The key of E is great because we can use the open strings of the guitar when we solo.

The following example shows the lead sheet of a 12-bar blues sequence in E. You'll see that, again, the chords are all dominant 7ths and the sequence is: E7, A7 and B7. In a moment, when you play through the progression, you'll hear how the relationship between these chords feels the same as the blues sequence in A.

Example 1h

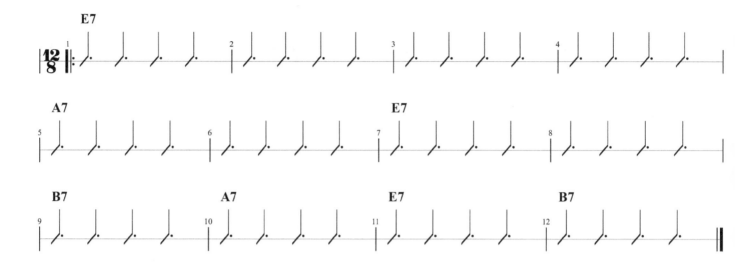

The next example teaches you the different chords you'll need in this key. Example 1i is played using all open chords. If you want to try barre chords, you can do so for the A7 and B7 chords. Play the A7 barre chord your learnt in Example 1c (with your index finger barring the 5th fret) and slide it up two frets to play a B7 (index finger barring the 7th fret).

Each chord is written as a being sustained for a whole bar, but I don't play the chords strictly as written on the audio track. Remember, the lead sheet is a guide to the chord lengths, not how to play them. Try to look ahead to see which chord is coming up, as this will help you change chords in time and keep the groove.

Example 1i

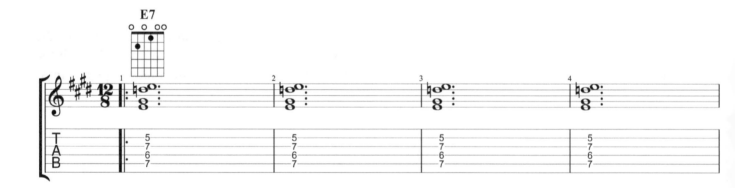

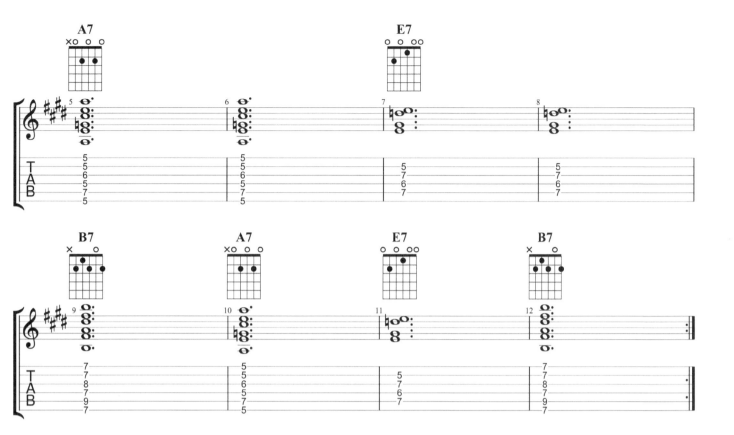

The rhythm part of Example 1j is virtually identical to the one you learned in the key of A, but the B7 is played as a single chord to give your fingers a short break and to avoid the large stretch that would occur if you were to stick to the same pattern.

Example 1j

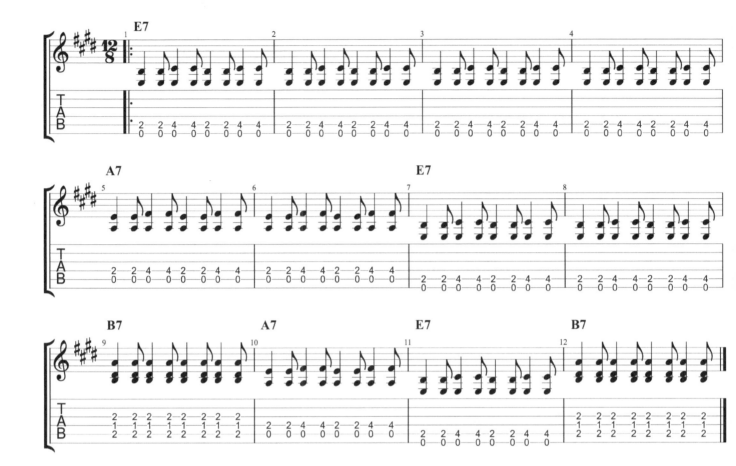

Here's a similar riff that gives your little finger a work out!

Example 1k

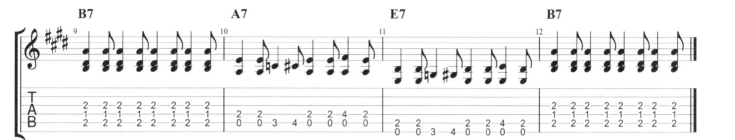

Finally, here's a riff that is reminiscent of John Lee Hooker's rhythm work. If you don't recognise that name, you'll definitely have heard his music. Hooker's tune *Boom Boom* from the early '60s album *Burnin'* has been used in countless films and TV adverts.

Example 1l

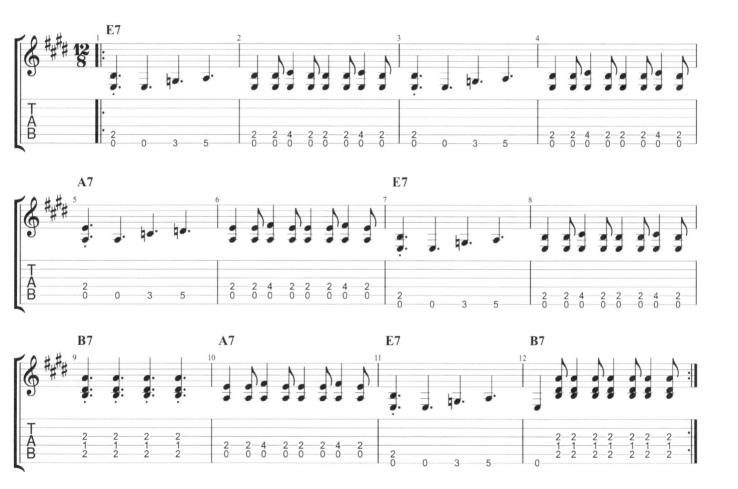

Memorise all the examples in this chapter before moving forward and make sure you can play a 12-bar blues rhythm part in the keys of both A and E.

In Chapter Two, we will begin our journey into blues guitar improvisation by learning the most important melodic sounds and scales used to create solos.

Chapter Two – The Minor Pentatonic Sound

The Blues isn't about knowing loads of theory, so the last thing I want to do here is to blind you with science. However, there is one scale you absolutely must know if you're going to play a good blues solo and that's the minor pentatonic scale.

Most scales in music contain seven notes, but the minor pentatonic scale contains just five. It doesn't sound like much when you first learn it, but with a few musical touches like bends and slides you'll quickly hear that it contains the very essence of the blues.

The A Minor Pentatonic scale can be played like this on the guitar (see diagram below). Can you see why it's often called the minor pentatonic "box" shape?

A minor Pentatonic

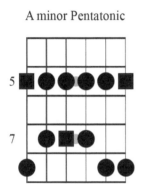

To familiarise yourself with the shape and sound of the scale, play it ascending and descending several times.

Example 2a

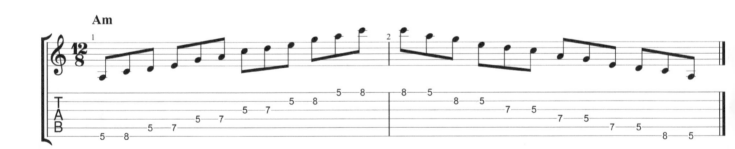

When you play the scale straight up and down it sounds kind of dull and not very bluesy. In fact, when you play it over an A7 chord like you learned in the previous chapter, one of the notes even sounds a little bit wrong! Don't worry, one of the most beautiful sounds in the blues is created when we "fix" this wrong note with a little bend.

I'm not going to fill this book with exercises, but one thing you should be able to do as a guitarist is play the following melodic pattern. This pattern will teach your fingers to move fluently through the scale while ascending and descending. If you can't play this yet, don't worry, just come back to this exercise later.

Example 2b

OK! Now it's time to get playing. These first few blues *licks* are very simple – maybe even a little bit dull! They contain no bends, no slides, no vibrato… nothing that would make them stand out as a beautiful phrase to wow your audience. However, they will teach you the *territory* you're going to use to make music. These licks are all in the key of A Minor, so first listen to the recording of each example, then play along with me before putting on the A blues backing track and playing them in time with the music.

Don't expect miracles, we're only in Chapter Two. See this as your chance to learn where all the important notes of the blues are. Notice that I don't play much on the bottom two strings.

Example 2c

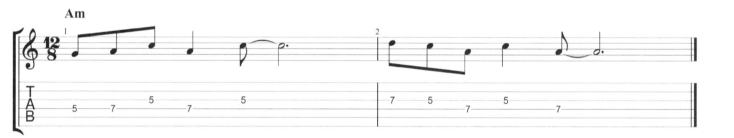

The next example uses a double-stop idea on the high E and B strings. This kind of idea was the staple of early blues and Rock 'n' Roll.

Example 2d

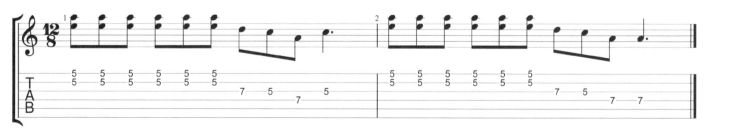

Now here's a repeating phrase.

Example 2e

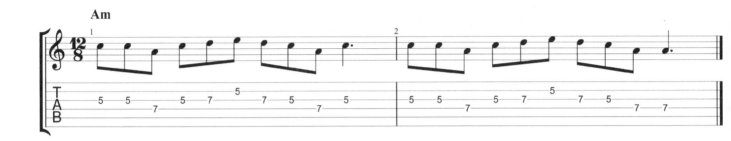

And finally, here's a lick that shows just how effective the simple five-note scale can be.

Example 2f

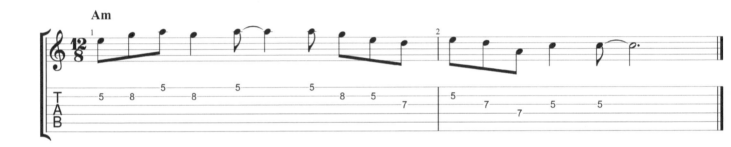

Now try playing your own short phrases over the backing track. See what you can invent. Don't worry about playing any "wrong" notes – just be creative.

And there we have it – everything you need to know to play the blues. Only joking, I'm sure you can hear that we're not playing cool solos yet!

So, if we know the right scale, and we are playing over the right chords, what is missing when it comes to playing blues guitar solos?

How about these ideas:

- Bending notes

- Rhythm

- Phrasing

- Dynamics

- Articulation

- Attitude

- An understanding of the language of blues guitar

There are seven important ideas here. In the following chapters I'm going to take a look at the first six in turn. We will see how they combine to help us discover the seventh – an understanding of the blues language.

Before then, we've still got a little bit of work to do to learn the minor pentatonic scale in the other most important blues key: E.

We've discussed how barre chords can be moved up and down the neck in order to change to different keys. The same is true of pentatonic scales. The A Minor Pentatonic scale began on the 5th fret, but if we slide it up to begin on the 12th fret it will now be in the key of E.

Here's how you play the E Minor Pentatonic scale

E minor Pentatonic

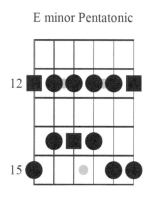

Example 2g

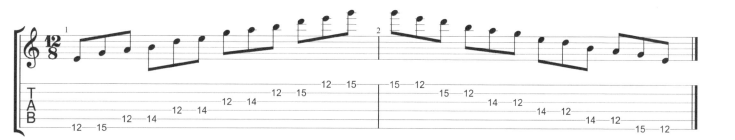

Here are a few simple (boring for now!) phrases that you can use to explore the E Minor Pentatonic scale. Notice that the rhythm is quite dull and there are no bends or exciting ideas. The only point of these ideas is to teach your fingers some of the *patterns* that are used in common blues licks.

Again, listen to my playing first, then play along with the recording before trying each idea on your own with the blues backing track in E.

Example 2h

Example 2i

Listen carefully to the rhythm of this next example on the audio download and copy it as accurately as you can.

Example 2j

The great thing about playing in the key of E is that you can use the open strings on the guitar too. In fact, you can move the E Minor Pentatonic down to begin on the open strings and play it as below. Use your third and second fingers to play the fretted notes.

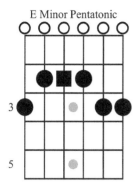

E Minor Pentatonic

Example 2k

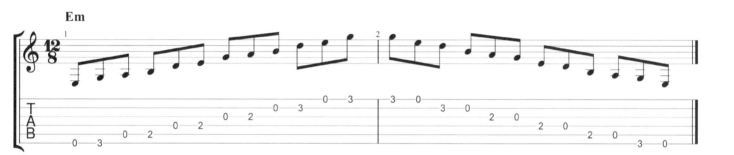

Virtually all great blues guitar players *love* using open strings in their playing. Here are a couple of ideas to teach you the territory of the open position pentatonic scale on the guitar. Listen to the recording first, play along, then play them over the E blues backing track by yourself.

Example 2l

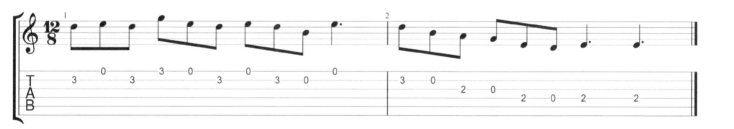

Example 2m

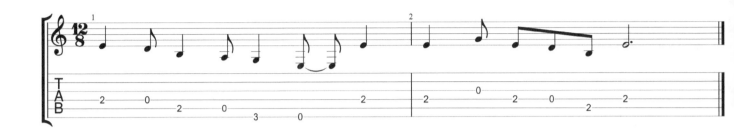

These licks aren't going to set the world on fire, they are just here to teach you how to use the territory of the minor pentatonic scale to make short blues melodies. We'll discover some more interesting licks later.

Make sure you can play the minor pentatonic scale up and down in the keys of A and E, and spend some time trying to come up with short little melodies over the respective backing tracks.

In the next chapter we will look at how you can add one magic touch to almost any pentatonic phrase to make it instantly more bluesy and musical.

Chapter Three - Bends

When you bend a string on the guitar you raise its pitch smoothly from one note to another and this mimics some of the nuances of a singer's voice. Remember, the blues is a music with its roots in Africa and was originally sung in the cotton fields and plantations before emancipation. It existed way before the guitar was introduced and copying this vocal style helps us to create an authentic language rich in cultural tradition.

To play a bend, fret a note normally, pick the string and then raise the pitch of the note by pushing your finger across the fretboard towards the bass strings. It's also important to *support* the bend by placing any spare fingers on the string behind the fretted note. This will lend a bit of strength and control.

Let's begin by looking at a few different bends before adding them into some blues licks.

To play the first bend, use your third finger to play the 7th fret on the third (G) string. Place your second and first fingers on the third string close behind the third. They'll probably both just about fit between the 7th and 6th fret.

Pick the string, then use your three fingers to push the string across the fretboard towards the bass string and listen as the note rises. We'll worry about how much the note should change later.

Example 3a

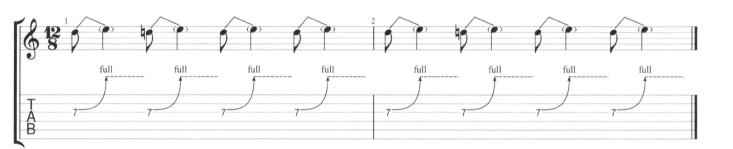

Now play Example 3a again, but this time bend with your second finger supported by your first finger. You'll probably find it a little more difficult.

Now repeat Example 3a, but this time use just your first finger. That's quite difficult, isn't it? Don't worry, we'll deal with this challenge later!

Once you can bend a note, the next question is, "How far should I bend it?" Let's begin by bending the note up so that it sounds identical to the note two frets higher. The distance of two frets on the guitar is called a whole tone.

In Example 3b begin by giving yourself a target pitch to aim for. Play the note at the 5th fret B string, then bend the note at the 7th fret on the third string until it sounds *exactly* like the previous note. Use your third finger and don't forget to support it with fingers one and two on the string behind it. Listen to the audio and you'll quickly hear what's going on.

Example 3b

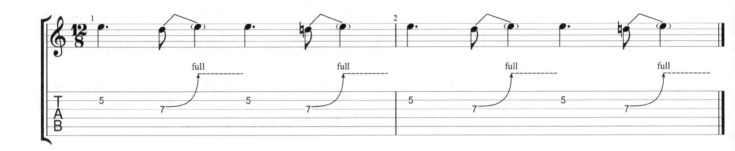

Try the same bend at the 7th fret and use the 9th fret for reference, as if you were playing the A Minor Pentatonic scale.

Example 3c

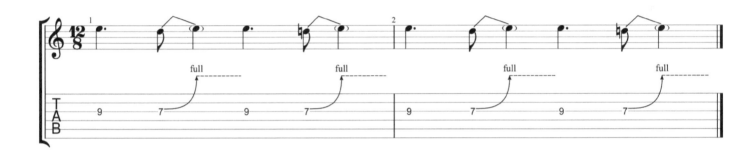

That's enough exercises for now – let's learn some simple blues licks that include a bend. To begin with, aim to play the bend as accurately as possible, but don't worry about that too much for now. The strength to play bends perfectly develops over time. As always, listen first, then play along with me before jamming with the E blues backing track.

This example shows a very common way of incorporating bends into a simple blues phrase.

Example 3d

Example 3e begins with another common bending technique. Bending the B string a whole tone from the 8th to the 10th fret changes a G note into an A note. The note played on the high E string, 5th fret, is also an A note. The notes "bounce" off each other and the overall effect has a vocal quality to it, like someone wailing.

Example 3e

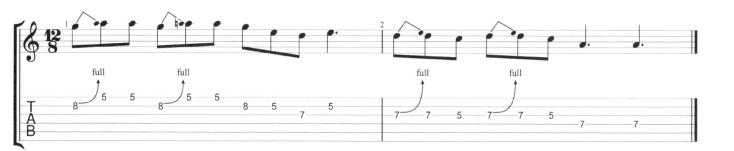

The next example is a must-know blues phrase. A common mistake for beginners is not to bend the note far enough in a whole tone bend, so that it doesn't quite reach the intended pitch. Keep in mind the note you are bending to. The first bend in this example is from a C note on the 8th fret to a D note. Play a D note first (high E string, 10th fret), to fix the pitch in your mind, then practise bending up to it from the 8th fret.

Example 3f

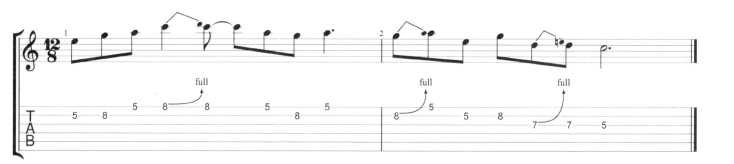

As you can hear, bends immediately add a vocal quality to the pentatonic scale and we quickly sound much more like a blues guitarist. However, we're far from finished with bending. As you'll see, there are plenty of ways to bend a note to give us unlimited creative potential.

Let's now introduce some smaller bends: the *semitone* bend and *microtone* bends.

Bending up a tone is great and you'll do this all the time, but the real emotion of a blues solo comes out when we add tiny bends to our phrases. In fact, many great blues players do this to almost every note.

Think about your speaking voice for a second. As you get more excited, generally the pitch of your voice will raise. As you relax, it returns to normal. But you definitely don't speak in a perfectly defined scale! The pitch of your voice just naturally *blends* between different notes without any effort on your part. To create an authentic blues performance, we want to copy this nuance on the guitar. To do this we can use tiny little bends that hint at, but don't quite reach the next pitch.

The next example shows the most common place to add a semitone bend to the minor pentatonic scale. Play it with your first finger. You don't have any spare fingers to support the bend, so pull the string downwards slightly towards the floor instead of pushing it up. It will help if you push the side of the first finger up into the bottom of the neck to act as a level.

Working with E Minor Pentatonic, begin by seeing if you can bend the 12th fret up by a distance of one fret (semitone) until it sounds exactly like the 13th.

Example 3g

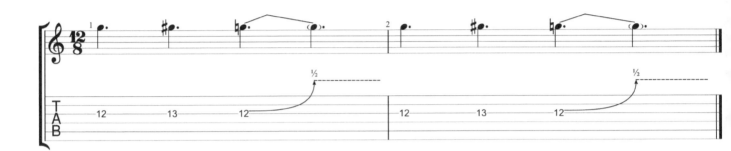

Next, bend the 14th fret up until it sounds like the 15th. This is a very special note in the blues and is given the name "The Blue Note". Listen to the effect it creates on the audio track. It's pretty much the most bluesy note there is and it's used all the time in blues guitar soloing.

Example 3h

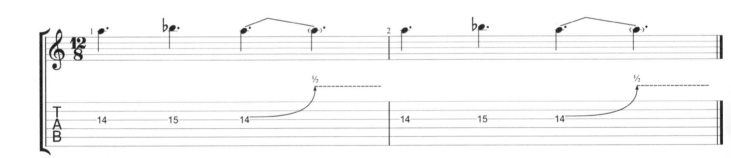

You've learnt to bend a note one semitone with the first finger. It's a nice safe bend that sounds great when used in the right place. Here are a few blues licks for you to practice that use semitone bends.

It can be tricky to switch between full and semitone bends with accuracy, so Example 3i is not only a cool lick but a great training exercise. It begins with a fast full bend, and has a soulful semitone bend before the end of the first bar. Can you hear how it hints at the pitch it's aiming for, but doesn't actually reach it?

Example 3i

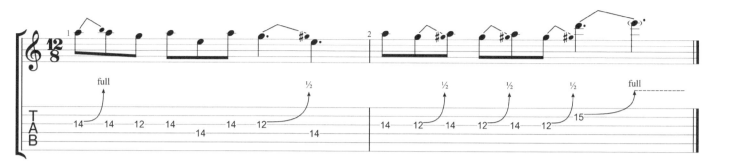

The semitone bends in the next lick really begin to bring out the vocal quality of the blues. Listen to the audio and copy my phrasing closely.

Example 3j

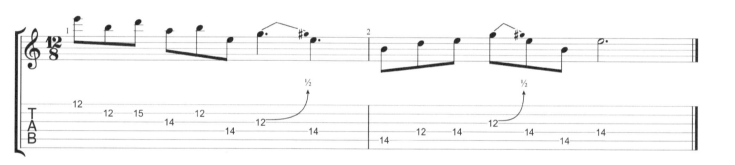

One of the tools blues guitarists use is *repetition*. This can mean repeating a phrase, or simply repeating a note a number of times to wring every ounce of soul from it. The next example uses a repeating phrase with a bend. Pick the note on the B string, 15th fret, then bend it up and immediately pick it again, before picking the note on the high E string, 12th fret (it's the same note). The result is a phrase that sounds the same note three times in quick succession.

Example 3k

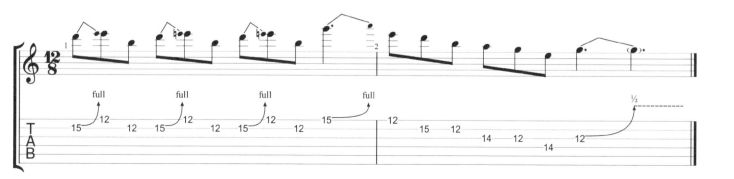

Now let's look at the *microtone bend*, which means bending any note less than a semitone.

Microtone bends are probably the most important expressive tool blues guitarists have in their arsenal.

You can read that sentence again if you like.

When I play the blues, almost every note is given a tiny, almost inaudible bend. That skill takes years to develop but I want to introduce you to it now because you'll immediately notice a huge jump in your soloing skill.

Until now, the bends we've looked at have been a set, defined distance – either one fret or two frets. Microbends don't have a defined distance. In fact, there are multiple pitches you could play before you even reach a one-fret bend.

To understand this, listen to the audio for the next example. I bend the 5th fret on the third string with my first finger, and see how many tiny pitch changes I can find before the bend reaches a semitone. Listen first, then see how many tiny incremental bends you can find between the 5th and 6th fret.

Example 3l

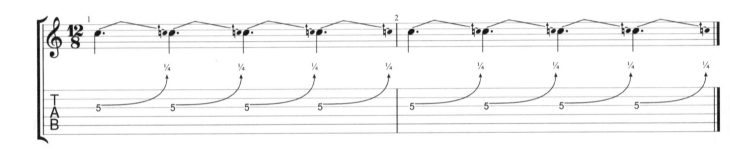

Let's learn some blues licks that contain microtone bends. These bends are normally called *curls* and are shown in the notation by a 1/4 bend sign. This doesn't mean that you have to bend exactly a 1/4 tone, far from it! The idea is to give the string a tiny little nudge in the right direction.

Before you play, listen to the audio, because these licks are all about nuance. Sometimes the bends will be slow, sometimes they will be quick. Listen carefully to see how each curl is performed.

Example 3m

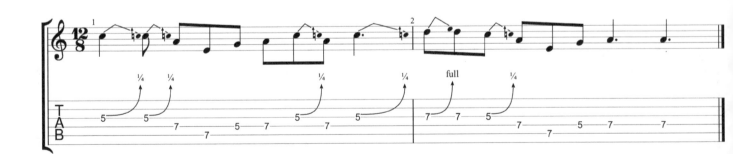

Here's another repeating note idea that uses a quick curl.

Example 3n

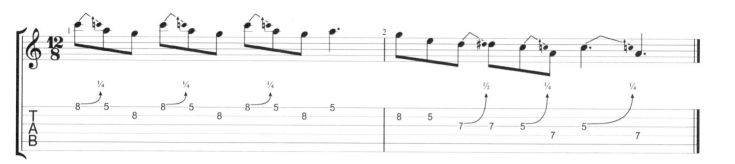

Example 3o combines full bends and curls to create expression.

Example 3o

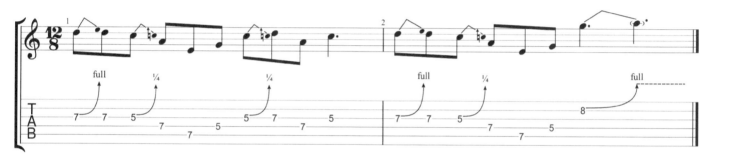

You may remember I said earlier that when you play a minor pentatonic scale over a dominant 7 chord (for example, A Minor Pentatonic over A7), one of the notes can sound a little bit wrong? Well, curls are the way to fix this problem.

I don't want to blind you with theory, but it's important you know this.

The chord of A7 contains a C# note, but the A Minor Pentatonic scale doesn't contain a C#. Instead, it has a C. When you're soloing, the C in the A Minor Pentatonic scale *rubs* against the C# in the A7 chord and creates *dissonance*, which can feel uncomfortable.

More often than not, soloists add a little curl to the C note to push it *slightly,* but not all the way up to C#. This technique *hints* at the "correct" note but rarely plays it outright. This little game is one of the most important sounds of blues guitar soloing and is one of the most important things to master in your playing.

Look back over the previous three licks and listen again to the audio. Can you hear where the C is curled up towards C#? (Hint, the note C is located on the third string, 5th fret, and the first string, 8th fret).

One thing you need to know is that often these little microbends or *curls* aren't notated in the music because they happen all the time and can be added to almost every note. With them, the notation would look a complete mess and be very confusing.

What this means to you when you're soloing is that you shouldn't be afraid to give any note of the minor pentatonic a little bend with your fingers. It works on pretty much any note except the root. The next lick combines whole tone bends and curls again. Pay careful attention to their execution and as always, listen to the track before playing along.

Example 3p

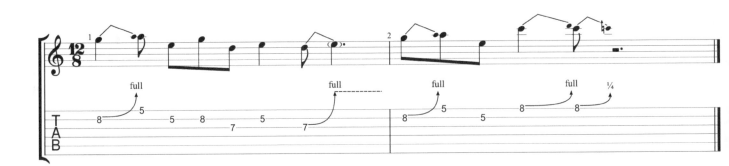

In the next example, the two quickly executed microtone bends add real groove to the feel of the phrase.

Example 3q

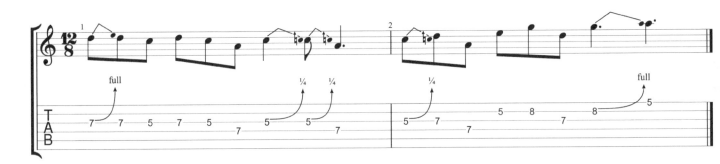

The next lick combines all three types of bend: whole tone, semitone and curl. Listen to how expressive the phrase becomes in bar 2 as semitone and curl bends alternate.

Example 3r

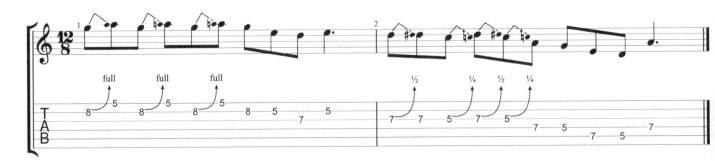

Now try beginning each of these licks in the 12th fret position to play them in the key of E. This process is called *transposing* and it's an important skill for all guitarists. Guitar licks work like barre chords – you can move them up and down the neck to play them in different keys.

Now it's over to you. Memorise the licks you've learnt in this chapter, put on the blues backing track and play each lick when you feel like it. You'll quickly find that you've put together a simple blues guitar solo.

Here's one way you could put these licks into a solo. As you learn more vocabulary, your solos will start to get more and more interesting. For now, focus on bending in tune and playing each lick confidently. If this solo feels like too much of a stretch at the moment, break it down into smaller sections – one bar at a time if you need to – and practise the individual licks. When you're confident with the licks, attempt the full solo.

Example 3s

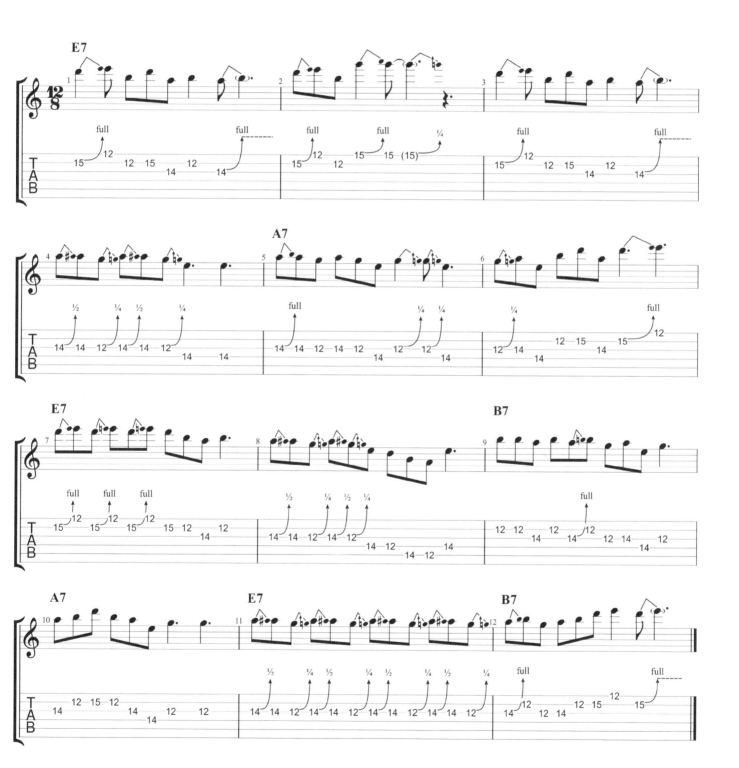

Creative and Emotive Bends

Before we move on, let's look at a few more ways we can play bends on the guitar. These techniques can be very powerful when done right and used naturally in a blues solo.

The first idea is called a *pre-bend*. This is where you bend the string up *before* you pick it. Once you've picked it, you release the bend to its natural pitch. Pre-bends can be a challenge at first, because there's no audible reference for how far to bend the string. Try playing the target note before playing the pre-bend as we did earlier and you'll soon learn how far to bend the string so that it's in tune.

The following example includes two pre-bends. Look for them in the notation and listen carefully to the audio.

Example 3t

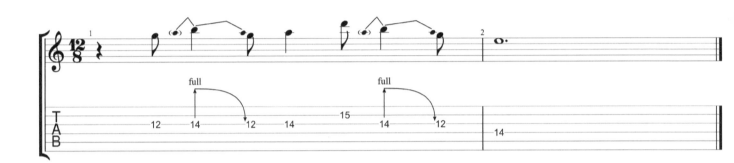

Another approach used by many blues players is to bend a string up and pick it repeatedly while holding the note. Often you'll speed up or slow down your picking as you do this. In the following example, play the start of the lick and then bend the 14th fret up by a tone and gradually slow down as you repeatedly pick the bend. It's essential to listen to the audio here, because the timing is all about feel.

Example 3u

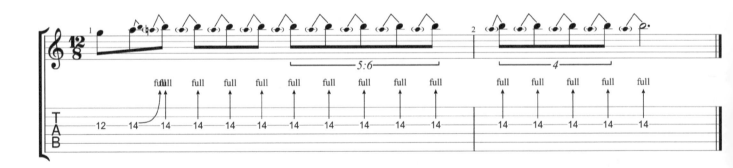

Following on from the previous idea, try playing the same lick and then releasing the bend as you pick it.

Example 3v

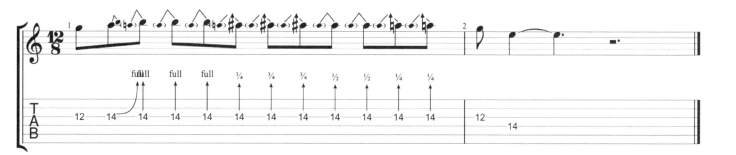

Another great idea is to bend a note, release it, then bend it up again but not quite as far. Bend the note on the G string, 14th fret, up a tone, release it back to the start position, then bend it up again by a semitone. Jimi Hendrix often bent notes like this to create a *crying* type effect.

Example 3w

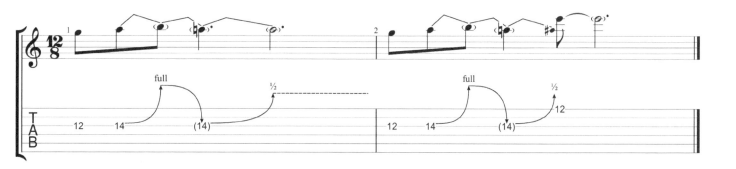

If you're feeling brave, now try the opposite approach: perform a smaller whole-tone bend on the 15th fret of the first string, release it, then play a bigger tone-and-a-half bend on the same note.

Example 3x

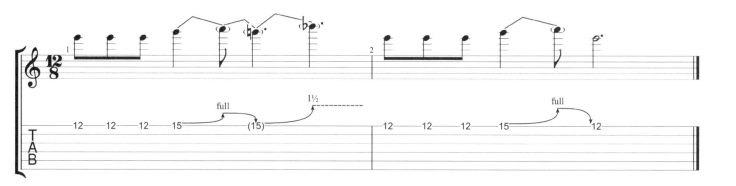

Now it's time to jam along with the backing track and practise introducing these exciting bending techniques into your playing. Don't worry about making mistakes – it's all part of the learning process.

Now we're getting to grips with bending notes, in the next chapter we'll examine the next piece in the puzzle of playing blues guitar solos – rhythm.

Chapter Four – Rhythm

OK, I know this is a beginner's soloing book! I don't want to bore you (and the stuff I'm going to teach you in this chapter might seem a little bit theory-based at first) but if you stick with me I'll show you an absolutely incredible way to think about blues soloing that allows you to be creative and not so reliant on licks.

Don't get me wrong, learning a lot of blues licks is an important part of becoming a good blues guitarist – you need to understand the language of those who have gone before, so your playing is authentic and sounds as it should. You'll learn more than I could ever teach you by breaking down the language of your favourite players, transcribing it, then learning to play it. There will be plenty more licks in this book so don't worry.

However, one phrase you may have heard is, "It's not what you play, so much as *when you play it*." This is true and is a very important feature of blues guitar playing. Think about this: we've already learned the most important five or six notes from which 90% of all blues solos are created. Doesn't it make sense that it's *how* and *when* we play those notes that sets us apart as musicians?

To understand this, I'm going to take you on a quick journey of rhythm. When we're done, you'll have a much better understanding of how rhythm in the blues (and all music) works. Your sense of time (rhythm) will be much better and, more importantly, you'll be able to place any guitar lick exactly where you want in order to play some pretty powerful stuff. In fact, you'll be able to play any lick in hundreds of different ways, just by thinking about rhythm. This material is a little advanced, so stay with me. I promise it is worth your while and will make you a much better player.

Ready? Let's go.

Look at all the earlier musical examples in this book and you'll notice there is a symbol saying 12/8 at the beginning of each line (see below). This is the *time* signature. I won't bore you with the theory, but it means that each bar (or measure) of music contains twelve 1/8th notes. That might sound weird, but it's just a little quirk of music.

You probably know that that there are four strong *beats* in each bar of music and these are accented by the kick and snare of the drummer. Listen to the blues backing track and hear how the drummer divides the bar into four.

Now listen to the cymbals. Can you hear how they're grouped in threes? There are three cymbal hits (or implied hits) on each beat of the bar. You should be able to count **1** 2 3 / **2** 3 4 / **3** 2 3 / **4** 2 3 / throughout the music.

4 beats per bar and 3 subdivisions per beat = 12 divisions per bar. That's where the sign 12/8 comes from.

Let's play every single one of those divisions on the guitar. Look at the notation part above the tablature and you'll see that there are four groups of three in each bar.

Example 4a

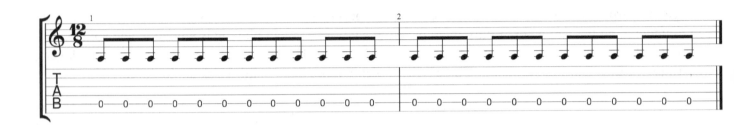

I appreciate that this isn't very inspiring right now, but we're getting there.

Now let's play a note that lasts a full beat, followed by a group of three notes. Listen to how I give one note a little curl to make it sound more bluesy. I even add a bit of *vibrato* to make everything sound a little more vocal. (We'll learn about vibrato and other dynamics soon).

Example 4b

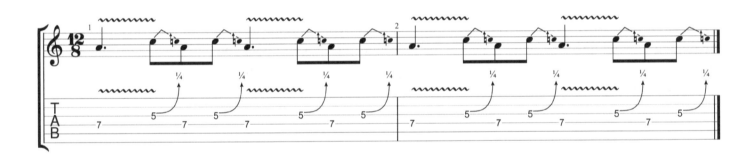

It's not jaw dropping, but we're definitely closer to playing some decent blues vocabulary. Here's a similar idea that ends with a long slow bend. Again, I add a bit of vibrato to make it more musical.

Example 4c

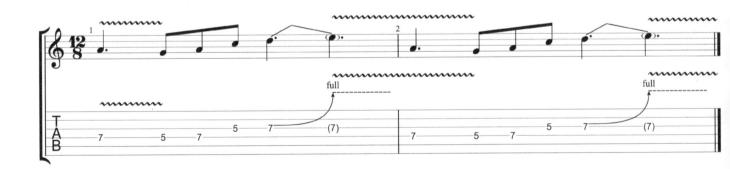

There's nothing here that you don't already know. I'm playing the pentatonic scale, adding a couple of bends and thinking about rhythm.

Now, let's introduce some silence into our lines.

The best way to make people listen to you is to only speak when you've got something meaningful to say. Often, if you're quiet and only speak when you have something important to say, the people around you will really sit up and take notice. The same is true in music. It's very easy to switch off when someone is playing a million notes per second, but if you keep your audience waiting for your next blues lick, you'll build tension and create a more powerful solo.

The next line is a similar phrase to before, but this time I don't play anything on beat one.

Example 4d

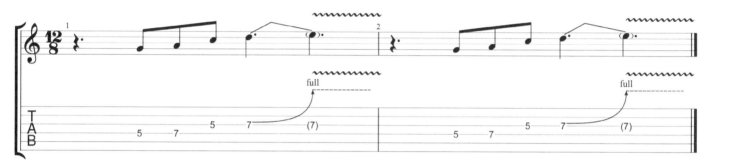

Now I rest on beats one and two.

Example 4e

Now here's a longer line that's built from two different phrases. Notice how I create a bit of tension by avoiding playing on beat one in the second bar.

Example 4f

The musical term for what we're doing is called *placement*. I'm being extremely deliberate about where I place each note and phrase. This is one of the secrets of good blues soloing. As you'll soon see, we can be *very* selective about where we place each note.

Here's an exercise you can work on to improve your rhythm and placement. Using the notes of the minor pentatonic scale only, play short phrases that use *only* the following rhythm. You can play any scale notes or bends you like.

Example 4g

Now, keeping the rhythm identical, solo over the blues backing track in E, beginning the phrase on the first beat of the bar every time. Here are the first few bars as an example.

Example 4h

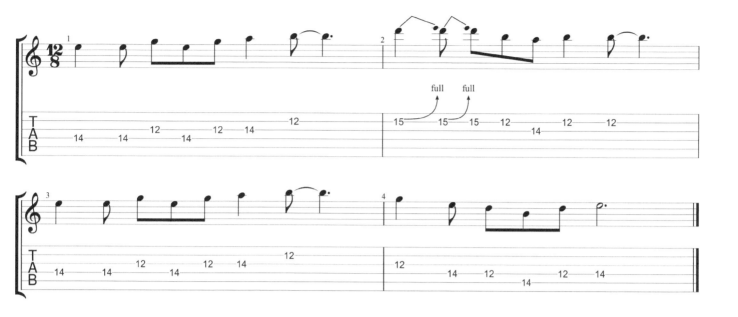

This time play the same rhythm but begin the phrase on beat two each time, like this.

Example 4i

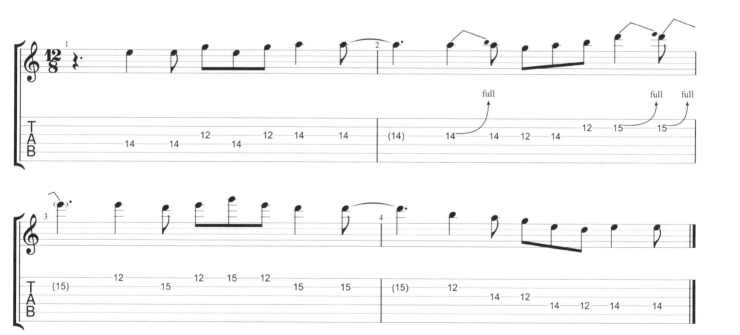

Repeat this to begin on beat three and beat four of each bar.

When you've done that, come up with another rhythm and repeat the exercise until you're confident in beginning a phrase on each beat of the bar.

Now let's move on to some more interesting rhythms.

We now know there are three divisions of each beat in the bar. Let's "tie" the first two notes together while keeping the third to create an important bouncy rhythm in blues guitar soloing. Listen to the following example before playing it.

Example 4j

Here's the same rhythm played around the pentatonic scale. Listen to the little bends I add in as standard, and how I phrase the lines as a question and an answer. When we tie two notes together like this, it's great to play them as a bend. (This is just an idea, there are no hard and fast rules).

Example 4k

Now let's reverse the rhythm and tie together the final two divisions of the beat. Here's that played around the pentatonic scale.

Example 4l

Playing one rhythm for too long can quickly get boring. In the next example I combine the previous few rhythms. Remember, I'm not really thinking about "licks" here. I'm just thinking about rhythm, but you can hear it's already beginning to sound pretty bluesy.

Example 4m

Go back through the previous few rhythms and use them to explore the notes of the A Minor Pentatonic scale over the A blues backing track. When you're ready, think about being silent for the first beat of each bar and gradually increase the amount of silence you include. Notice how your licks start to jump out.

Use your ears to help you find an *answering* phrase for any musical *questions* you ask. Don't worry too much about the quality of your lines right now, remember we're just discovering how rhythm works. When you've mastered this, you'll have a huge amount of freedom to play every lick you ever learn in a million different ways.

We've looked at how the three 1/8th notes in each beat can be combined to build interesting rhythms and phrases, but what if we want to play a little faster or squeeze a few more notes into each beat?

The next rhythmic level is created when we *divide* each of the 1/8th notes in half, thereby doubling the amount of notes we play. When we split an 1/8th note in half, we create two 1/16th notes. In the following example, I split the third 1/8th note of each beat into two 1/16th notes. It feels like a nice, natural phrase, even though I'm just playing up and down the minor pentatonic scale.

Example 4n

Here are a couple of phrases that use this rhythm more creatively. I've not isolated the rhythm, instead I've used it in a lick that immediately combines some of the rhythms we've looked at so far.

Example 4o

Example 4p

Here's an idea that doubles the second of the three 1/8th notes to create a driving line. Learn it first by playing down and up the minor pentatonic scale.

Example 4q

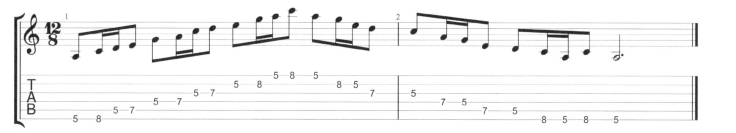

Here's that idea combined with other rhythms in a more traditional guitar lick.

Example 4r

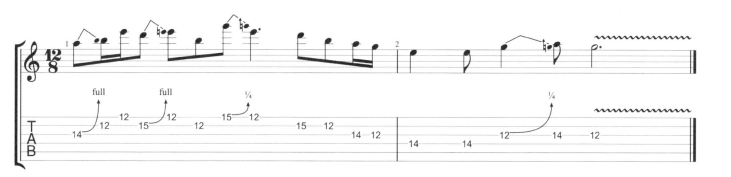

Finally, let's subdivide the first of the three 1/8th notes in the beat. Learn it with the minor pentatonic scale first.

Example 4s

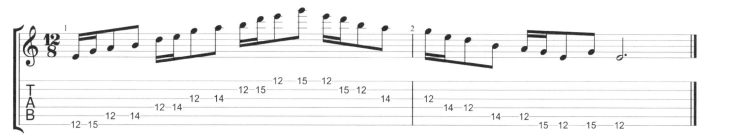

Now here is a lick that uses this rhythm.

Example 4t

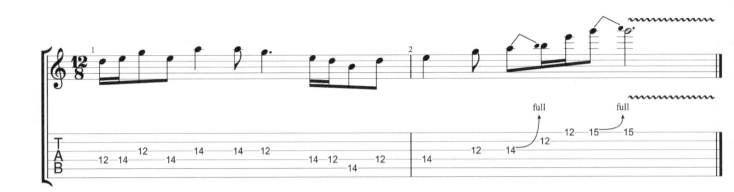

Take each of these rhythms in turn and play each one for a few minutes over a blues backing track while exploring the minor pentatonic scale. Add bends and try to create musical phrases. Begin to deliberately combine them, two at a time, and see which ones sound good together. Gradually, begin to introduce rests (silence) and create short phrases that are surrounded by silence. Think "question and answer" and gradually add in longer, slower notes to build meaningful phrases.

Example 4u shows how I combine two 1/16th note rhythms with rests and longer notes over a 12-bar blues in E. Remember, I'm not really thinking "licks" I'm thinking of rhythms, exploring the pentatonic scale, and using question and answer phrasing.

You could spend days, weeks or months practising ideas like this, and when you begin to combine this kind of exercise with some of the licks you already know, you'll quickly find your playing getting more and more creative, while naturally emulating the players you love.

Of course, you could split two, or even all of the 1/8th notes in the beat in half, and as your solos begin to build in intensity, you'll find yourself naturally including more of these rhythms. Generally, leaving space and playing slower rhythms will create a more relaxed solo that will gain in intensity as you begin to play more notes... but not always!

Here are a few blues licks that use more 1/16th note divisions. Memorise them and play them over the backing track in E.

Example 4u

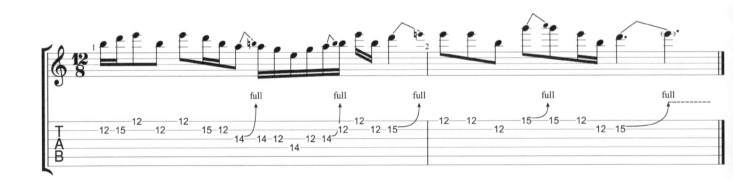

Example 4v

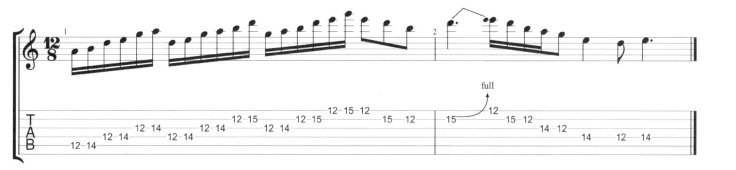

Example 4w

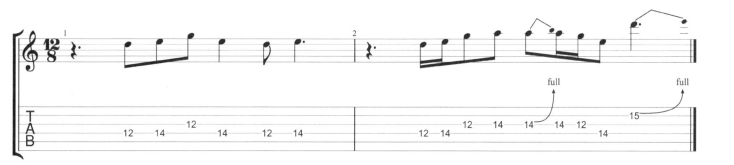

We've covered a lot of ground in this chapter. I want to conclude with a few final thoughts.

The reason we've been discussing rhythmic divisions is because it's important to understand how rhythms work together to build a great solo. Strong rhythms, with good bends and dynamics, will *always* build strong phrases that connect with your audience.

When I'm onstage, or jamming with a friend, I'm certainly *not* thinking "Okay, I'll play this rhythm with a 1/16th note division on beat three, then I'll play…" that would be ridiculous. However, by finding a strong phrase and *developing* it rhythmically, I know that my solo will always be well structured and powerful.

Another reason is that you need to have *heard* and *played* these rhythms to understand them and introduce them into your playing. By working through these rhythmic ideas you will begin to build your vocabulary. You've been introduced to these ideas logically and musically, so they should start to gradually creep into your playing.

One thing I see in my beginner students is the tendency to "explore" the minor pentatonic scale when they're first asked to improvise a blues solo. It's a real turning point when they realise that they already know all the right notes and that they make better music when they start *exploring rhythm* instead. All good music is based around great rhythm, groove and phrasing. We all have the same notes, it's how and when we play them that sets us apart as musicians.

The take-away idea is to start with a strong rhythm in your first phrase. You don't really need to think about the rhythm of the second phrase you play, because the musical part of your brain will take over and naturally suggest an answering phrase. That's the beauty of the blues – everyone has this ability.

To demonstrate, here's a simple 12-bar solo that I improvised around the strong rhythm I play in the first bar of the song. The solo never goes too far away from this rhythm, and I only use notes of the minor pentatonic scale in the melody. The solo is in the key of E, so learn it slowly then play along with the backing track.

Example 4x

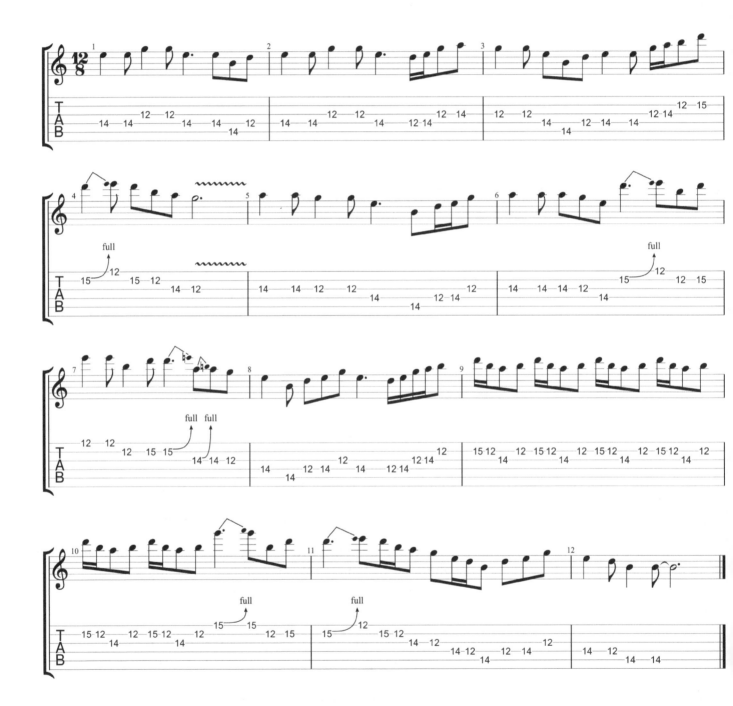

The following chapters contain multiple licks and ideas. I won't talk too much about the rhythms they use, but I want you to look at the notation and see how the lines are constructed rhythmically. You won't see many rhythms that haven't been covered in this chapter, no matter how advanced the licks become. That alone should tell you that rhythm is paramount.

By working through this chapter, you've opened up your ears to new rhythms and creative possibilities that we'll combine freely in future sections.

Chapter Five – Vocal Vibrato, Sexy Slides and The B.B. Box

So far, we've looked at the most important scale in blues guitar soloing, how to add bends and how to use rhythm to drive a solo forward, but you may have noticed that your licks begin quite abruptly and, when they end, they fall slightly flat and the energy tails off. In this chapter, I'm going to teach you how to make your phrases sound a bit more human.

Say the word "Hey!" out loud and listen carefully. Also pay attention to the physical feeling of creating that sound. Can you feel the slight increase in energy in your throat as you begin to speak? How about the "H" forming in your throat and gradually getting louder until the word appears? Then, there is the strength of the word itself and finally a little tail off when the "ey!" dies in the roof of your mouth.

To add a more vocal quality to their playing, blues guitarists mimic these physical characteristics at the beginning and end of their licks or phrases.

How, you might ask?

At the beginning of the lick we can add a little *grace note* – a slide up from nowhere into the first note, to create that activation energy in the voice.

At the end of the lick we can add some *vibrato* – rapid, repeated bends that create a wobble on the note, which mimics the decay of the voice as it fades to nothing at the end of a sentence.

Slides and vibrato are often overlooked by beginner guitar players but are some of the most personal nuances we can give to our playing. In fact, many great guitarists can be identified by their vibrato alone. There are as many different feels of vibrato as there are players, and once you've mastered the technique you will naturally use it to add your own personality to your solo without even thinking.

By now, I'm sure you're eager to explore a little bit more of the guitar neck, so we are going to learn a new soloing position on the neck. We'll work in the key of A for now, while I introduce you to a very important area to solo in: *the B.B. box*. The B.B box is named after blues legend B.B. King, who was very fond of soloing in this position. As you might imagine, a huge number of blues licks and vocabulary can be found by exploring these notes.

Example 5a

The B.B. box is a cool hybrid of major and minor pentatonic scales, built around a root note played on the 2nd string with your index finger. Unlike the minor pentatonic, which is defined by its b3 (C) and b7 (G), the major pentatonic is defined by its 3rd (C#) and 6th (F#) – and both major and minor tonalities are available in the B.B. box.

Here's the full box pattern of notes B.B. King would play. Just remember, this isn't a scale you'd play, but a selection of notes to draw from. Learn the pattern carefully, as all the licks in this chapter will be built from it.

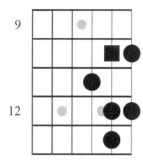

B.B. Box

Now we've got this important territory sorted, let's look at how to perform vibrato and slides before circling back and learning some iconic blues licks using this shape.

Vibrato

As described earlier, vibrato literally means to "vibrate" a note by adding a series of small, fast repeated bends, and it's one of the techniques that really helps to shape your personality as a guitarist. Your vibrato might take months, if not years, to develop and will change over time. While I appreciate that this is a beginner's blues guitar book, I think it's very important to become aware of, and start working on, your vibrato as soon as possible. Don't worry if it doesn't come quickly – it'll take time and any small amount of vibrato you create will dramatically improve your blues guitar soloing.

Vibrato can be performed with any finger, so let's begin with your first. Play the 10th fret of the second string with the tip of your first finger and gently push the side of your finger up against the underside of the guitar neck. This point of contact will act like a little pivot and your finger like a lever to gain a bit of mechanical advantage over the string.

Now, pick the note, wait for a second, then gently turn your wrist outwards to pull the pitch of the string slightly sharp. The back of your hand should move very slightly towards the headstock of the guitar while the side of your finger pushes up into the underside of the guitar neck. If you are playing right on the tip of your finger, you'll find that this lever action pulls the string slightly downward towards the floor, and the note goes slightly sharp.

Immediately relax your wrist and the string should return to pitch. Repeat the movement several times. Try to increase the speed at which you wobble the note but remember, the movement comes from the wrist and the finger should pivot against the bottom of the neck. The finger itself shouldn't be what's creating the movement by bending. The movement can be compared to turning a key in a lock.

Vibrato is shown in notation by wavy line after a note. A thick wavy line shows that the vibrato should be wide and pronounced. A thin wavy line means that it should be subtle and light.

The following example demonstrates the instructions above. I pick the note, hold it for a beat, then add a light, slow vibrato.

Example 5b

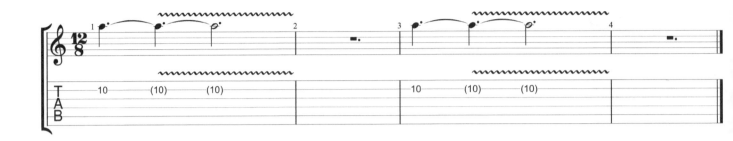

Here's the same example, but now I add a thicker, faster vibrato after two beats.

Example 5c

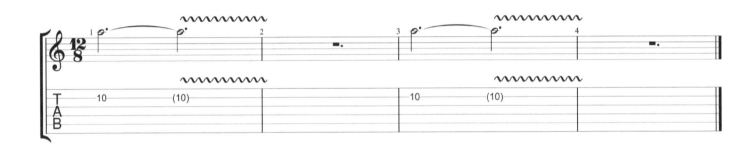

Now let's add some vibrato with your second finger.

Play the 12th fret on the third string and place the first finger on the string directly behind the second finger, just as you would for a bend. Again, pick the note, wait a beat, then add some vibrato. Remember that the movement comes from the wrist, not the finger.

On the track I add a medium/fast vibrato.

Example 5d

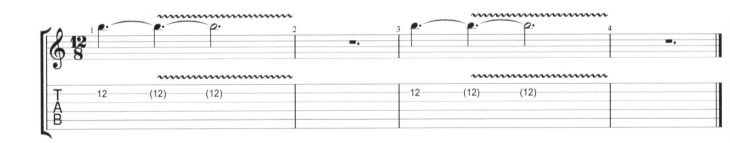

Finally, let's add vibrato using our third finger. Pick the 13th fret on the second string and add vibrato after a beat or two. Here I add fast narrow vibrato after two beats.

Example 5e

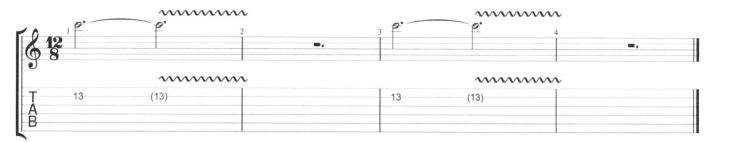

Vibrato can be added to a bent note too, but the technique is a little harder and will take some time for you to master. Until now, we've been playing a note, then repeatedly bending it slightly sharp. However, if you've bent a note, it's difficult to bend it any further and keep it in tune, so when we add vibrato to a bend, we bend up, then slightly lower, then re-raise the note to the bend repeatedly.

To demonstrate, I'll bend the 12th fret note up by a whole tone (this note is that major 3rd we talked about earlier), then add vibrato to the bend by repeatedly lowering and returning the bend to pitch.

Example 5f

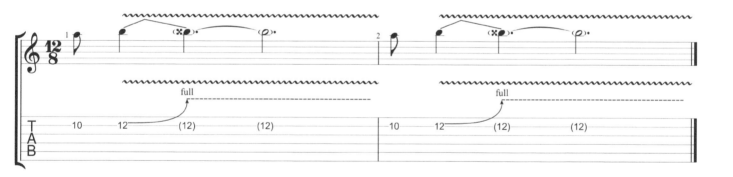

As mentioned, your vibrato might take a while to develop but it's an exceptionally important technique to master. Not only does it lend a vocal character to each note, it helps the note to sustain for longer and makes your playing a lot smoother.

Sliding In

Before we begin learning some licks, let's quickly take a look at how to *slide* into a phrase. You may have played slides on the guitar before and you probably know that it's relatively easy to pick one note then slide up or down to the next one.

What we're going to do here is add a *grace note* (almost instantaneous) slide just before the target note. You can actually make that slide as long or as short a distance as you like, but let's start with a slide that begins two frets below the target.

To play a grace note, place your third finger on the 13th fret and pick the string. As you pick the string, instantly and firmly slide your finger up the neck, coming to a hard stop on the 14th fret. If you're feeling brave, hold the 14th fret for a beat before adding a little vibrato.

Example 5g

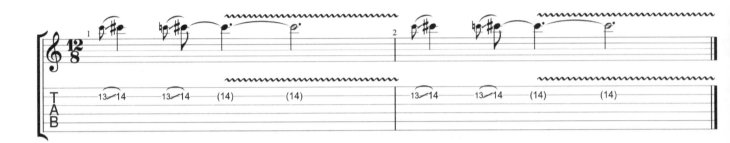

Now practise sliding into each of the notes of the B.B. box using all four fingers. The first time though, use your first, then use your second finger, etc. Finally, use your second finger to play the note on the third string, then your first and third fingers to play the notes on the second and first strings – just as you would if you were fingering the scale normally.

Example 5h

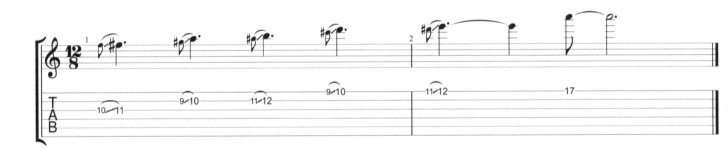

Next, repeat the exercise, but instead of sliding into each note from one fret below, try sliding from much lower on the neck – maybe around the 3rd fret. What you'll find is that your fingers need to start moving *before* you pick the string. Listen to the audio to see how this sounds and feels.

Example 5i

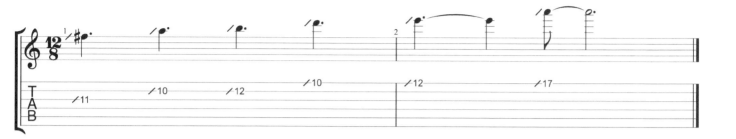

I know you're eager to get going but I want you to learn the final technique of sliding *out* of a phrase after you've added the vibrato. This is exactly the same as sliding into a note and it's just another way to add a bit more musicality and nuance to your playing.

After the vibrato, relax your hand while keeping the finger lightly in contact with the string, and slide down the guitar neck towards the first fret. Again, how far you travel has a subtle effect on your phrase.

This example demonstrates how I slide into a note, add vibrato, then gently slide off to nothing. I'll play the note without any of the above techniques first, then play it again with the slide in, vibrato and slide out. I'm pretty confident I know which one you'll prefer.

Example 5j

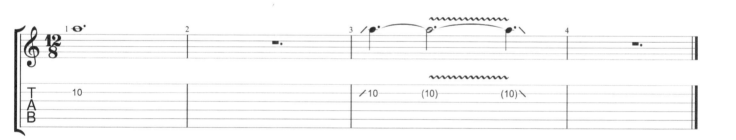

It's often said that you can identify a great blues guitar player by them playing just one note. I'm sure the example above shows you exactly why that's true.

B.B. Box Licks and Solo

OK, enough technique. Let's learn some excellent blues licks this new pattern. In each one, I slide into the phrase, add vibrato in one or two places, and slide out of the phrase to finish. Try playing the licks without these little flourishes and you'll hear how dry they can sound. These licks are all in the key of A.

As always, listen to the audio first, learn to play them, play along with my recording, then try them out with the backing track. Don't be afraid to alter them by playing with the rhythm or melody to make them your own.

Example 5k

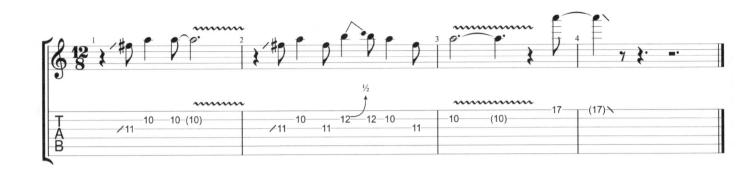

Example 5l

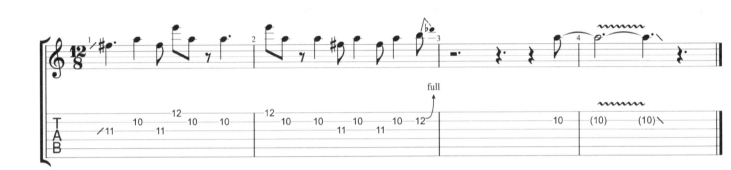

Example 5m

Example 5n

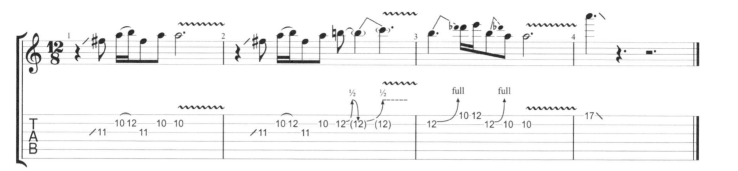

Example 5o

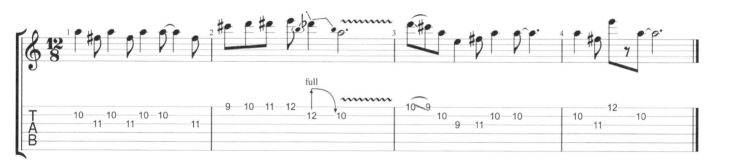

As you know by now, playing a blues guitar solo is all about context, not just about learning licks. Here's a 12-bar guitar solo that combines these ideas freely. I don't play each one exactly as written, but you should be able to hear how some of this vocabulary *influences* what I play.

Learn the solo and use it as a starting point to create your own ideas using the backing track in the key of A.

Example 5p

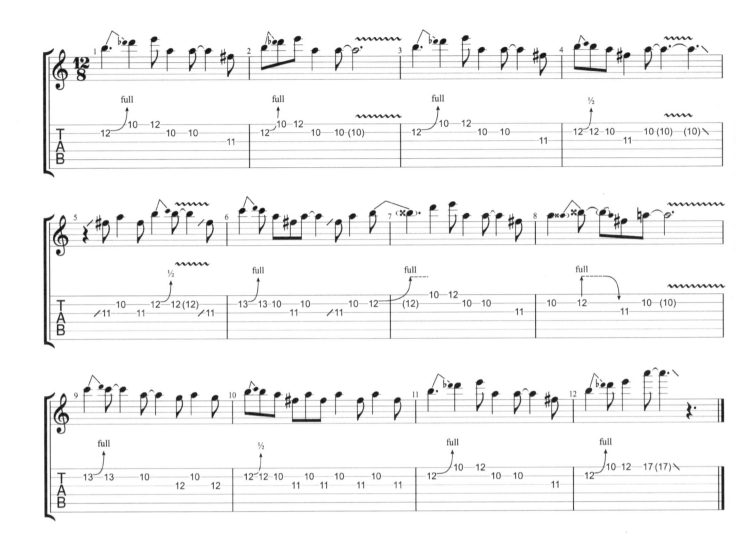

Finally, let's talk a little more about dynamics. We've already seen how little slides and vibrato make a world of difference to just a few notes, but there are other things you can do to really make your blues licks pop out at your audience and heighten the emotion.

One of the least talked about factors in playing a blues lick is how you pick it. Some players pick hard, some pick gently and some players even use their fingers or a combination of pick and fingers. Each of these factors affects the dynamics of your line in different ways.

Have you ever been in a room with someone giving a speech, or listened to a teacher speaking, where the person uses a continuous monotone? The lack of dynamics in their voice causes their lecture to get boring very quickly, even if they're talking about something quite interesting. As humans, we tend to switch off from a monotonous voice tone. The same is true of the guitar. We're often guilty of playing phrases using the same attack throughout and this can get dull for the listener really fast.

The following is one of my favourite exercises to help students rapidly develop their picking dynamics.

Set your amp so the tone is just on the edge of breaking up with distortion. Turn off any backing tracks so it's just you and your guitar.

Now, using only four notes, begin to improvise a solo while picking as quietly as possible. Listen to how your amp and guitar react to your pick dynamics. Very gradually, start to pick harder. Imagine you've turned up the volume of your picking hand by 10%. Keep playing for a few minutes, then turn up your picking hand by another 10%. Rinse and repeat until you're picking as hard as you possibly can. By limiting your solo to just four notes you can really focus on the dynamics of your picking hand, but don't forget to add bends, slides, vibrato and interesting rhythms.

Next, I want you to find as many different ways as you can to pick a single pentatonic line. Try beginning quietly and getting louder and vice versa. How about playing everything quietly except for just one or two notes? Try picking some notes with your fingers and some with your pick. Experiment with slow and fast vibrato and short and long grace note slides.

Use the following four-note lick to practise with and see if you can find 20 different ways to articulate the phrase using volume and dynamics. I'll play it in a couple of different ways on the audio track so you can hear what I mean.

Example 5q

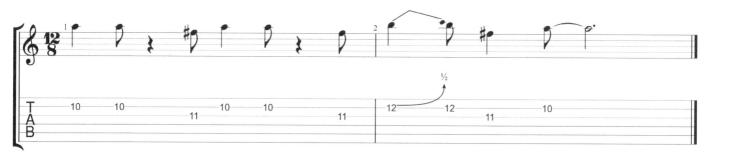

Another thing to experiment with is the angle of the pick as it strikes the strings. If you point the pick right down towards the floor and push hard, you'll get a bit of a delay and a "thunk" as the note sounds. If you angle the pick so it's completely parallel to the guitar string you'll get a lot of attack and "snap" on the note.

Again, take a single lick and see how you can alter the pick angle throughout the phrase to add new nuances to your phrases.

Another important technique to learn is *legato* (hammer-ons and pull-offs). Here, instead of picking every note, you only pick one note and use a fretting hand finger to sound the next.

The following example demonstrates how to play a hammer-on. Begin by playing the 5th fret on the third string with your first finger. Pick the note, then use your third finger to hammer down onto the 7th fret. Do this quite firmly and hold the hammered note down so it can ring out. Accuracy is important as you don't want to accidentally hit the wrong string. Pay attention to how these techniques are notated so you'll recognise them later.

Example 5r

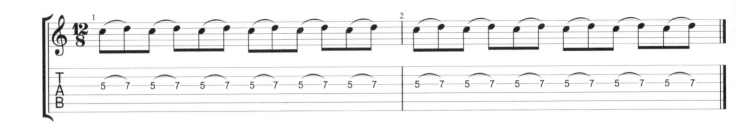

A pull-off is the opposite of a hammer-on. Play Example 5r again, but after you've held the hammer-on for a beat, pull the third finger down towards the floor so that it acts like a pick and sounds the 5th fret again.

Example 5s

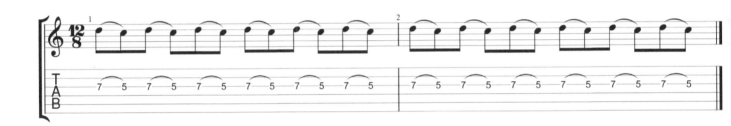

Now, try repeating this hammer-on and pull-off movement for as long as you can. The energy you give the note when you perform the pull-off should allow you to keep going until your hand gets tired!

Example 5t

Here are three licks similar to those you've learned before, rewritten to use hammer-ons and pull-offs. The *legato* markings are shown with a small curved line. Listen to the audio and hear how much smoother they sound when played with legato.

Example 5u

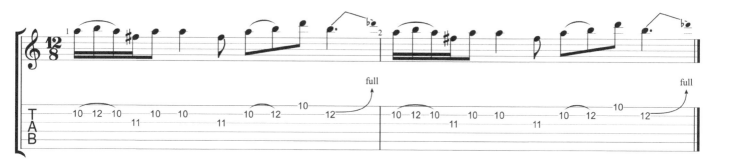

Example 5v

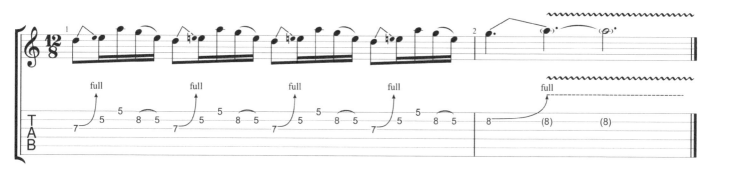

Example 5w

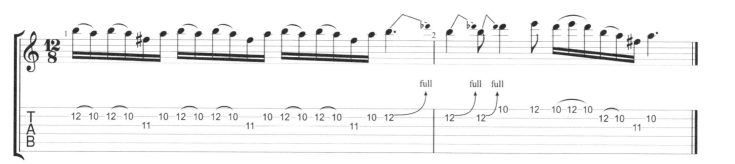

Sometimes you're going to want to play smoothly and sometimes you're going to want to dig in with the pick. Sometimes you're going to want to do both in the space of a few beats. It's really up to you.

Remember, we all have the same five notes, it's how and when you play them that sets you apart as a musician.

There are plenty of ideas in this chapter for you to play that will really help you find your own voice as a soloist. These ideas will take a lifetime to perfect but adding them into your playing now will help you to discover a deeper language that goes well beyond licks and scales. They can (and should) be applied to everything you ever play.

You're in the process of discovering how to create your own voice on the guitar, now let's move on and begin to open up some more of the guitar neck, to allow you more note choices and expression.

Chapter Six – Moving up the Neck

In the previous chapter we began to explore a bit more of the guitar neck by using the B.B. box in the key of A. In this chapter, we are going to look at a few more positions of the minor pentatonic scale and learn some important vocabulary around each shape.

The minor pentatonic scale can be played all over the neck, but some areas are better for making music than others. In fact, each area can lend itself to slightly different licks because the *intervals* of the scale are played in different locations. The concept of *range* (high notes and low notes) is important in music too. When we play in a higher register, this generally increases the sense of tension in the music, and when we play in a lower register it generally decreases the tension.

However, before we begin to explore the guitar neck, let's look at minor pentatonic shape 2, and learn to link them together

The scale shapes link together like a jigsaw. Here's a diagram of the A Minor pentatonic scale with shape 2 added on top. It's common to slide between these positions on the second and third strings.

Shape 1 and 2

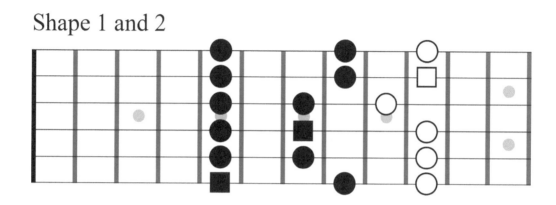

For example, I could move from shape one to shape two on the third string like this:

Example 6a

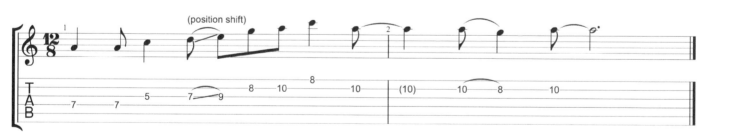

I'll let you explore all the different places you can slide up and down between these two positions.

The best way to learn how to link these shapes smoothly is to learn some licks that move between them, so now let's learn some vocabulary that links these shapes of the A Minor Pentatonic scale. Remember to add vibrato and slide in and out of phrases. In real life these won't always be notated in the score.

Example 6b

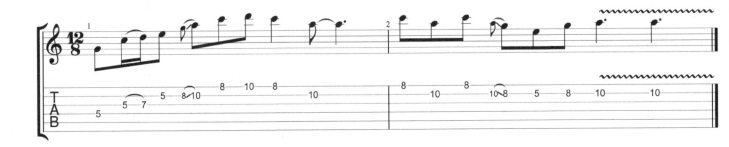

Example 6c

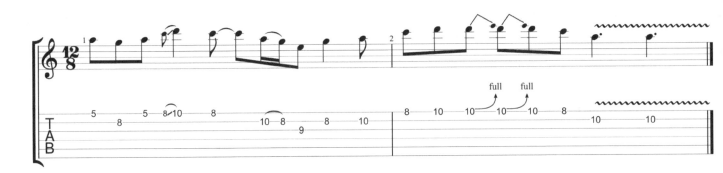

Example 6d

Example 6e

Now combine these ideas and create your own 12-bar blues guitar solo with them. When you're ready, transpose these ideas to the key of E and jam them with the E blues backing track. Here's a solo I composed to give you some ideas to start with.

Example 6f

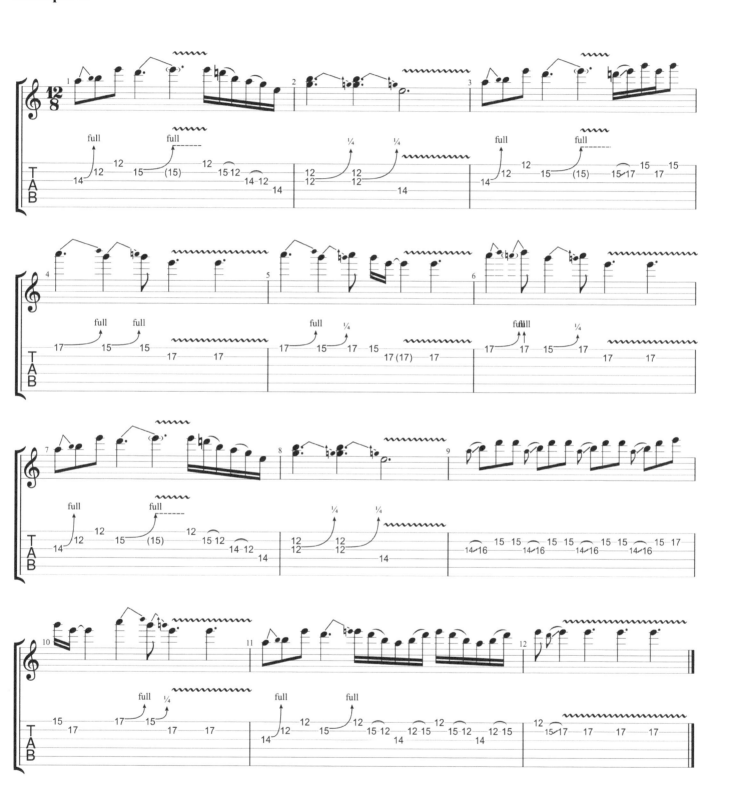

There are hundreds of common phrases you can play by using these shapes and moving between positions. Spend as long as you need to explore these shapes and copy the language of your favourite guitarists.

Now let's learn a few ways to move around the guitar neck confidently. We'll stay in the key of E because I first want to show you an important concept – how to play a lick an *octave* higher.

When a musician says that they will play a phrase an octave higher, it simply means play exactly the same notes at a higher pitch. That's quite easy on the guitar because all we need to do is move the lick 12 frets higher.

If you don't already know, the notes created by picking the open strings on the guitar are repeated 12 frets higher. Try picking the open third string, then play the 12th fret on the third string. You should be able to hear that these are the same note, one is just higher pitched than the other.

In the next example I first play a short lick using shape one of the E Minor Pentatonic scale that contains some open strings, then I play exactly the same set of notes 12 frets higher in shape one of E Minor Pentatonic at the 12th fret.

Example 6g

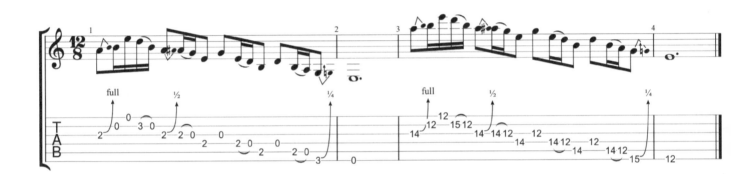

Here's another idea that I play high first, then drop an octave to play on the open strings.

Example 6h

This lick begins in shape one and slides up into shape two before being repeated an octave higher.

Example 6i

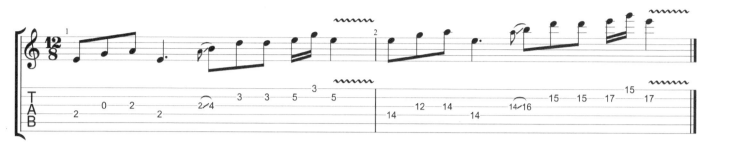

Of course, you don't have to play an identical line in different octaves, you can play the "question" in one octave and the "answer" in another. Here's a low question and a high answer.

Example 6j

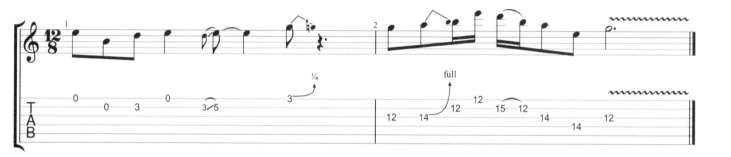

And here's a high question and a low answer

Example 6k

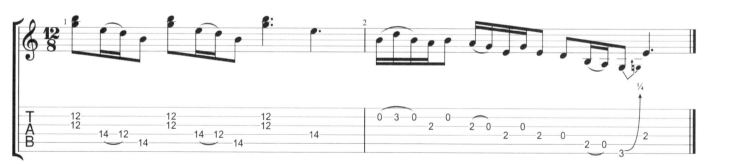

Being able to play a line in different octaves is extremely useful and is a powerful idea in the all-important question and answer phrasing which we will discuss more later.

Now write some of your own blues licks in the open position and play them an octave higher at the 12th fret. Begin by practising over the blues backing track in E, but then repeat the process in the key of A where you would begin around the 5th fret, then move each lick up to the 17th fret area.

Let's stay in the key of E a little longer and explore shape four of the minor pentatonic scale. It's a great shape to use as there are some lovely patterns and it's located quite centrally on the guitar neck, so you're not playing at some of the more the extreme ranges of the guitar.

E Minor Pentatonic shape four is played like this.

E minor Pentatonic

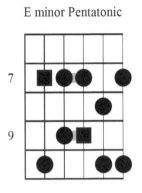

Example 6l

The area we are mainly interested in is located on the top four strings. The following five licks are fairly simple but will teach you some of the best ideas accessible in this position. Notice that I'm including a few 1/16th note phrases, a little legato, slides, vibrato and bends. Listen to me playing these licks along with the backing track then learn them yourself, trying to match my phrasing.

Example 6m

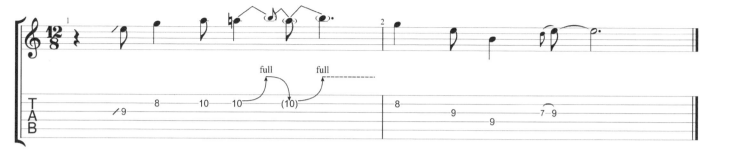

Example 6n

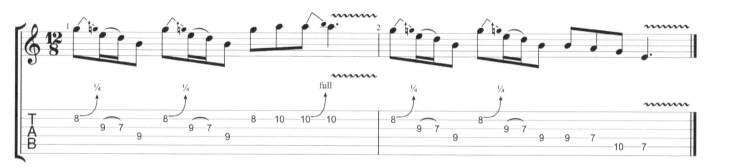

Example 6o

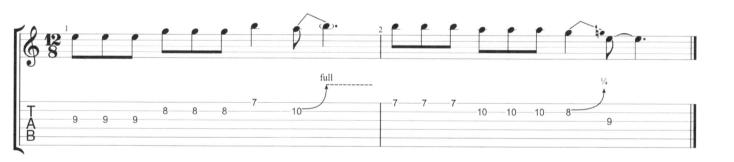

Example 6p

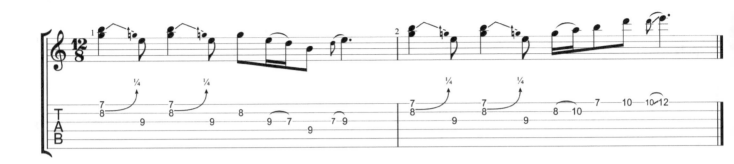

Now, here's a 12-bar solo in E using just shape four licks linked by a couple of connecting ideas. Pay attention to the articulation and try to match my phrasing on the recording.

Example 6q

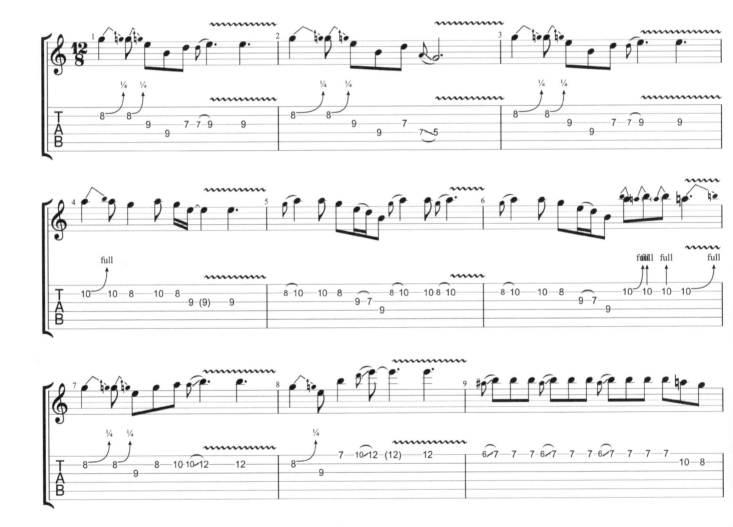

Now that we've got vocabulary in a few different locations on the guitar, here are some longer lines that connect all four.

In this example I start in the open position before moving up through position two, four and back to position one at the 12th fret.

Example 6r

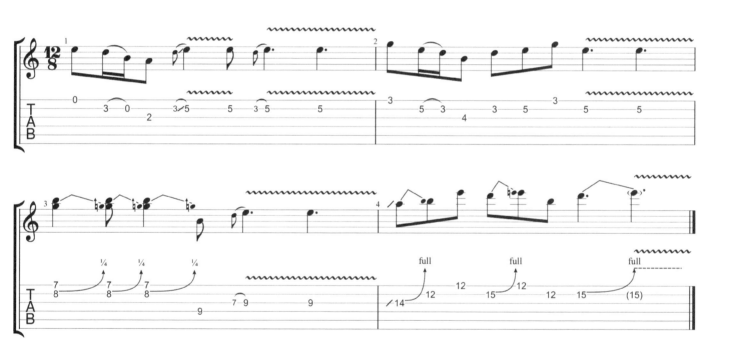

Next, I do the opposite and begin in position two at the 15th fret and work my way down to the open position.

Example 6s

Using this approach, it's easy to play one lick in three different *registers*, as in Example 6t.

Example 6t

Now it's your turn. Put on the E blues backing track and work your way up and down the guitar neck using licks you've already learnt in each position. Listen to how the tension in the music changes as you ascend and descend.

You can spend months exploring the guitar like this and creating hundreds of different lines, and I highly encourage you to do so. Listen to your favourite guitarists and try to hear how they navigate the neck.

The next stage is to repeat the process in the key of A. You have learned licks around the three pentatonic shapes in the key of E, so it's up to you now to transpose them to the key of A.

To help you, here's a diagram of the A Minor Pentatonic scale on the neck with just the parts we've covered highlighted in black.

A minor Pentatonic

Put on the A blues backing track and practise moving between these shapes.

You may be wondering why I've not covered shapes three and five. It's because the scale fragments I've covered are the most useful areas to help you develop great blues phrasing. It's better to focus on a small area of the guitar and get great phrasing, than to get bogged down in scale positions and technique.

Your phrasing will stay with you for life, and it's easy to apply great phrasing to new scale shapes later.

We've done a lot of work so far with the minor pentatonic scale, so in the next chapter we're going to discover a completely new sound and work with the *major pentatonic scale*. This sound was a particular favourite of Stevie Ray Vaughan and creates a much lighter, more chilled approach to the blues.

Chapter Seven – The Major Pentatonic Sound

Whereas the minor pentatonic scale has quite a dark, brooding sound, the *major* pentatonic is light, airy and somewhat happier. Both can be played over most blues 12-bar blues progressions and in this chapter we're going to explore some important major pentatonic language you should know.

There's a weird and unique quirk in music that, despite the major pentatonic sound being almost completely the opposite feel and vibe to the minor pentatonic, they can both be played with exactly the same fingering.

The classic trick when learning the major pentatonic scale on guitar is to slide shape one of the minor pentatonic scale down the neck.

To demonstrate this, I'll play E Minor Pentatonic starting with my first finger at the 12th fret. Then, I'll move that whole shape down three frets so that now my *little* (fourth) finger is placed on the 12th fret. I'll play this over the E blues backing track so that you can hear the difference in the sound of the two scales.

Example 7a

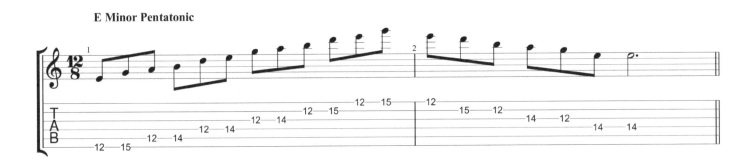

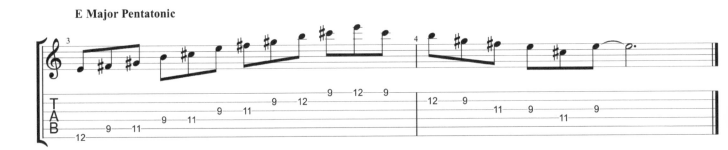

One important musical trick to take away from this simple concept is that many of the E Minor Pentatonic blues licks you already know can be shifted down three frets to become E Major Pentatonic licks. I say *many* rather than *all*, because certain notes you might bend will sound a little off. My advice is to use this trick as a starting point and let your ears guide you as to what sounds right. You'll soon learn to make small adjustments, so that your major pentatonic licks really "sit" with the music.

To get you started, here are some examples of minor pentatonic ideas that I shift down three frets to create major pentatonic licks. I might not play the major idea exactly the same as the minor idea, because sometimes the lines need to resolve to a different place musically.

Example 7b

Example 7c

Example 7d

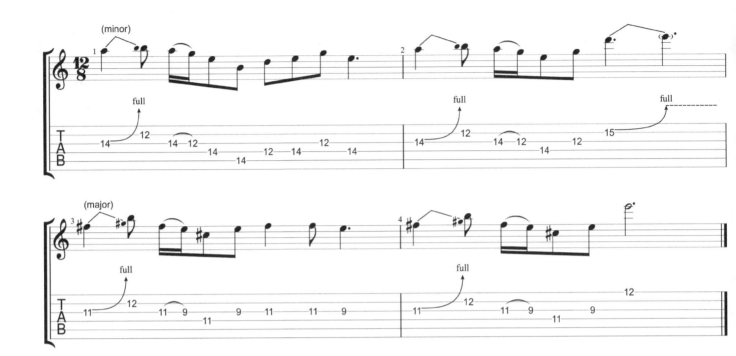

A little side note: often it's a much stronger musical strategy to *begin* with a major pentatonic idea, then shift it up three frets to turn it into a minor pentatonic idea, but we'll address this later.

While we are working in this position of the major pentatonic scale, here are three classic blues licks you should know around this shape. Stevie Ray Vaughan was a big fan of this shape and you can often hear it in his playing. Check out *Lenny* from his iconic album *Texas Flood* to hear the major pentatonic scale at its best. It's wonderful to hear how masterfully he switches between the major and minor pentatonic scales during phrases. See if you can pick them out.

Example 7e

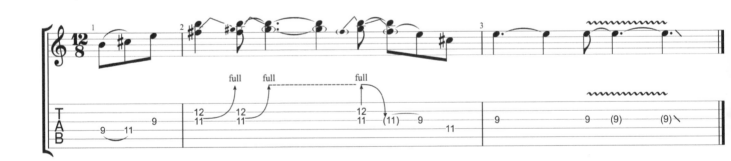

Example 7f

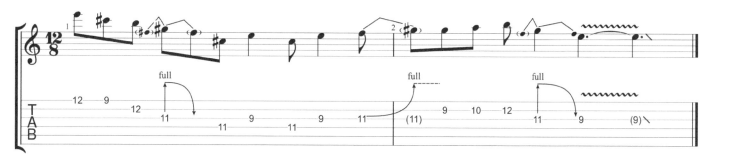

Example 7g

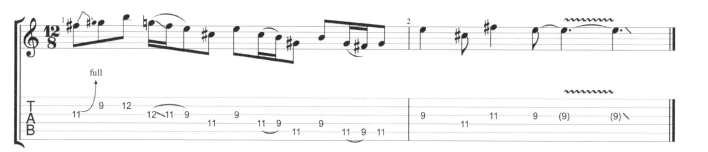

When you've mastered these ideas, try moving them all up three frets and playing them as minor pentatonic licks. Remember, they won't be perfect, you'll want to tweak the endings a bit to come back to E, but you have a great starting point!

Now you're starting to get a bit of a grip on major pentatonic language, let's look a bit deeper.

While we can happily play major pentatonic ideas by using the minor pentatonic shape three frets lower, this can be somewhat limiting. Instead, it's important to learn the major pentatonic scale in the same position as we originally learnt the minor pentatonic scale i.e., at the 12th fret in the key of E. The good news is that you already know the scale shape because it's the same fingering as minor pentatonic shape 2, just with a different root note.

E Major Pentatonic

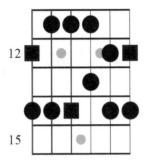

Example 7h

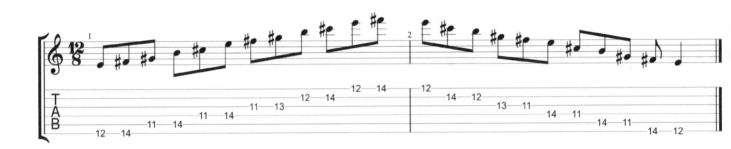

Here's some handy vocabulary you should know in this position. I'm very fond of playing *double-stops* (sounding two notes at once) and hammer-ons in this position.

Example 7i

Example 7j

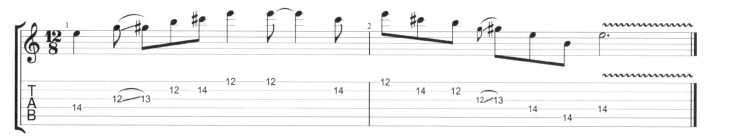

Example 7k

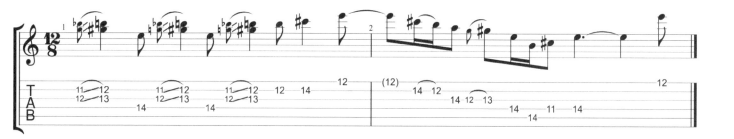

Next, I'm going to show you the most ground-breaking idea I ever learnt about playing blues guitar. When I discovered this concept, my playing just went into orbit.

While we can play both major and minor pentatonic licks, the truth is that the best blues vocabulary is a combination of both these sounds blended together.

Let's look at what happens if we superimpose the major pentatonic (hollow notes) on top of the minor pentatonic (black notes) scale.

Combination

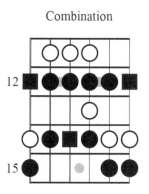

Can you see that almost every major pentatonic note can be bent up by a semitone to become a minor pentatonic note? This is huge. Let's explore this idea.

Here's a simple line that focuses on bending the first string 14th fret (major pentatonic) up to the 15th fret (minor pentatonic). Add some vibrato and listen to how fantastic this sounds.

Example 7l

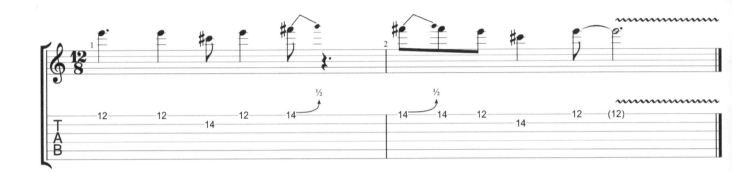

An almost identical line can be played in the same way on the second string. Notice that I drop down to the major pentatonic 13th fret note on the third string.

Example 7m

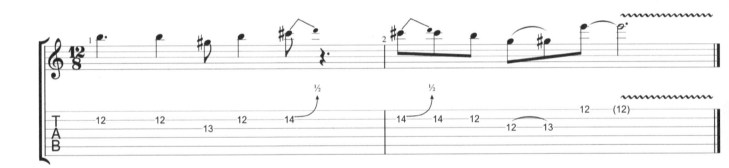

Here's a similar idea, but now focusing on a bend from the 12th to 13th fret on the third string.

Example 7n

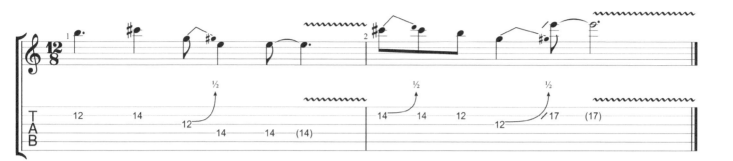

This combination of minor and major leads to one of the most common movements in blues. The next lick demonstrates a hammer-on from the minor note G on the 3rd string to the major G# a semitone above. You'll hear this idea used all the time now that you're aware of it.

Example 7o

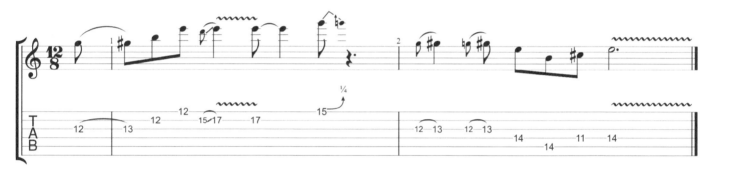

Here's another idea based around a major to minor pentatonic semitone bend at the 14th fret, followed by a minor to major semitone bend on the 15th fret.

Example 7p

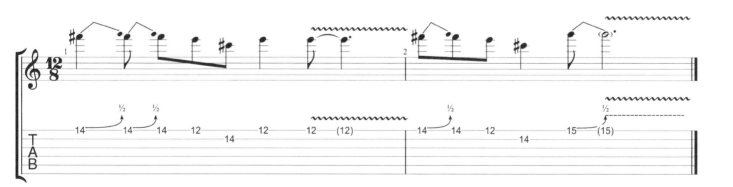

The next lick bends the major pentatonic note on the third string 11th fret up to the minor pentatonic note a semitone higher. It finishes by bending the 12th fret minor note up a semitone to the major 13th fret note.

Example 7q

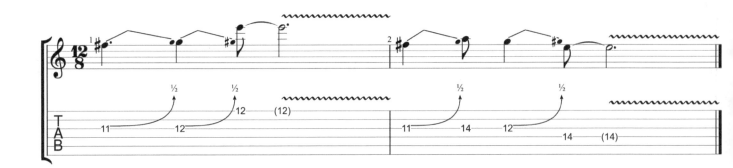

Here's a line beginning with a minor to major bend on the 12th fret before descending the minor pentatonic scale and sliding down to the major note G# on the fifth string.

Example 7r

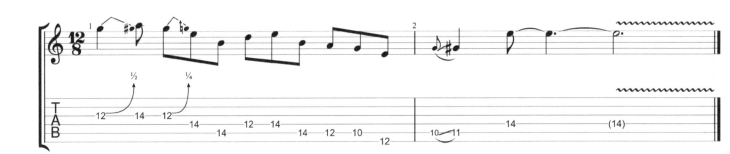

Play all of these ideas over the E blues backing track and explore as many was as you can to transition smoothly between these two scales.

To hear this process in action, here's a 12-bar guitar solo for you to learn that focuses exclusively on this movement between major and minor pentatonic scales around the 12th fret position.

Example 7s

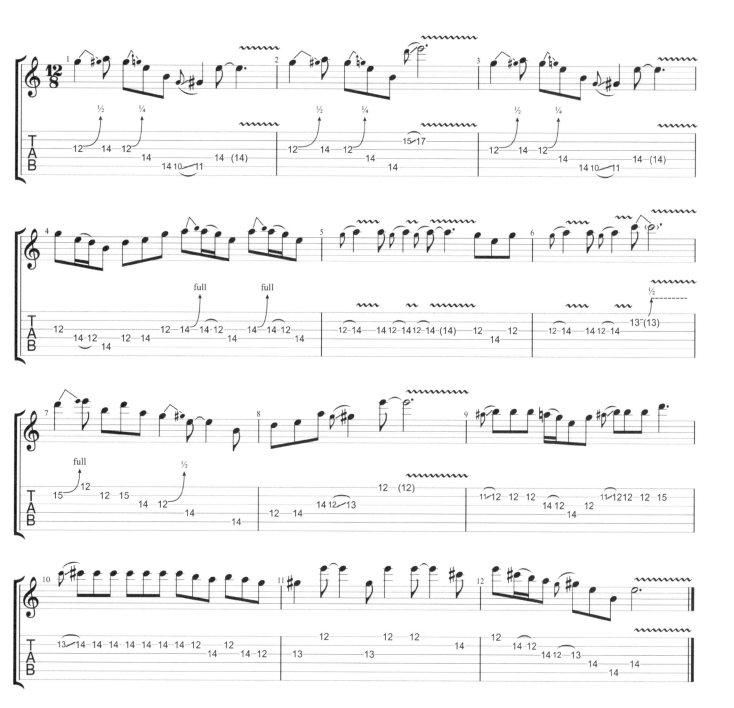

All too often I hear guitarists play exclusively major or exclusively minor pentatonic soloing ideas. What I've tried to show you here is a much more fluid, musical approach to blues soloing that helps you control the *mood* of your solo and to never run out of ideas.

We will talk about soloing schemes later, but for now, why don't you experiment by putting on a backing track and structure your solo by first playing a major pentatonic lick, moving it up three frets to play a minor pentatonic lick, then playing a lick that blends major and minor pentatonics by bending from one note to another. Suddenly you're playing well formulated ideas that have a strong musical foundation. This goes way beyond simply regurgitating blues guitar licks and helps you to take control of your solos. Remember to practise the same concepts in the key of A.

Chapter Eight – Highlighting the V Chord

Every single lick and idea we've covered so far will work at any point in the 12-bar blues, but when it comes to the V chord of the blues progression, blues musicians will often play something different to highlight it.

What is the V chord? It's the chord located five notes above the key centre.

In the key of A, count up five notes and you reach E:

A B C D **E**

So E7 is the V chord in the key of A.

In the key of E, B7 is the V chord:

E F# G A **B**

That's all the theory you need to know.

Refer to the lead sheet below (in the key of E) and you'll notice that the V chord (B7) occurs in bars nine and twelve.

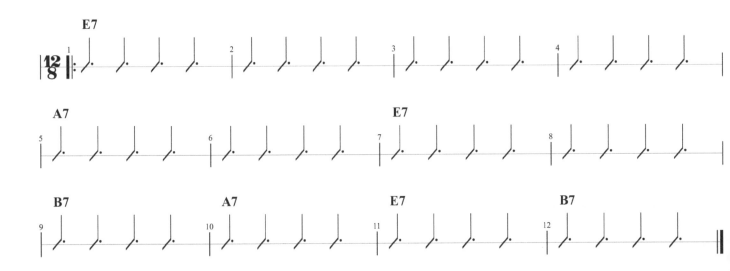

What's so special about this chord? In music, the V chord always wants to resolve to the I chord of a key (the I chord is the name of the key you're playing in). B7 strongly wants to resolve to E7 in the key of E. The V chord creates a tension that is released when we play the I chord.

Bar nine is the beginning of the blues progression "turning around", so it's often the high point in a solo, before the tune goes back to the top and you express a new musical idea.

Often, you'll be playing a *turnaround* idea in bar twelve, which we'll address later, but for now let's focus on what you can play on the B7 chord in bar nine.

The simplest approach is to continue to play major or minor pentatonic lines over the B7. These ideas work really well and there's absolutely nothing wrong with them. This is definitely language you should know and master.

Listen to the following lines. The first is an E Minor Pentatonic lick played over the B7 and the second is an E Major Pentatonic lick.

Example 8a

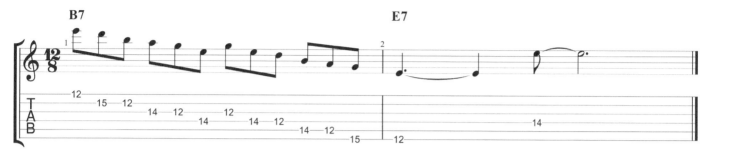

Example 8b

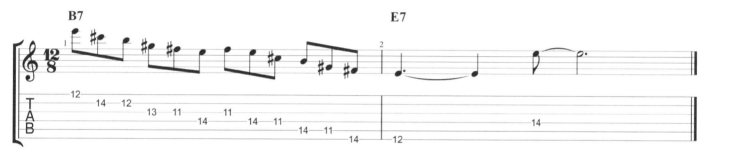

Of course, any lick that *combines* major and minor pentatonic ideas will work well too. Your ears will gradually learn to pull your fingers to the right notes on the B7 chord.

However, we don't *have* to use these ideas and sometimes it's nice to *highlight* the B7 chord by playing a B Major Pentatonic idea at this point in the progression.

One way to play the B Major Pentatonic scale is by using the shape you've just learnt, but down at the 7th fret.

B Major Pentatonic

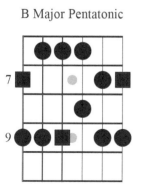

Example 8c

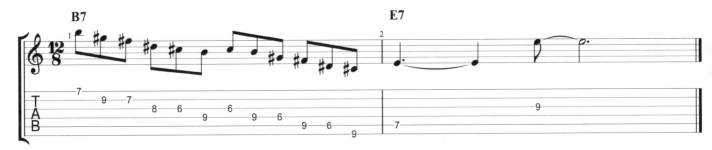

Here's a simple line that begins in bar ten (over the E7) with an E Minor Pentatonic idea, then outlines the B7 chord with a B Major Pentatonic idea.

Example 8d

Here are a couple more examples.

Example 8e

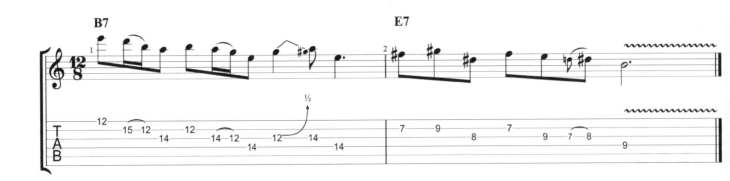

Example 8f

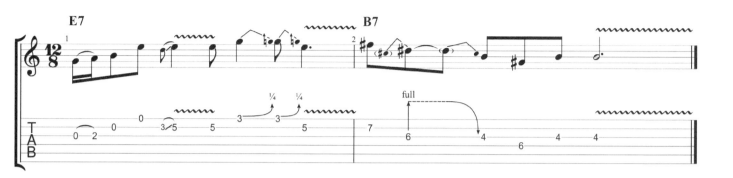

In fact, you can transpose any E Major Pentatonic or A Major Pentatonic lick you know into B and it will sound great at this point in the progression. You could even move a shape one B Minor Pentatonic lick down three frets as another quick way to access the B Major Pentatonic sound.

Look back at the 12-bar blues progression above and notice that the chord following the B7 is an A7 in bar 10. There's a great opportunity here, can you guess what it is?

An A7 is simply a B7 chord moved down a tone, so why not repeat your B Major Pentatonic idea a tone lower, to outline the A7 chord in the same way?

This approach can be a little predictable and formulaic, but there's nothing to say that you have to play exactly the same lick twice. You can vary the idea the second time you play it a tone lower. This all comes down to personal taste, so see if you like this approach. If not, E Minor Pentatonic still sounds great on the A7 chord.

Here are three licks that are built from playing B Major Pentatonic on B7, which is then shifted down a tone and repeated almost identically on the A7 chord. See what you think!

Example 8g

Example 8h

Example 8i

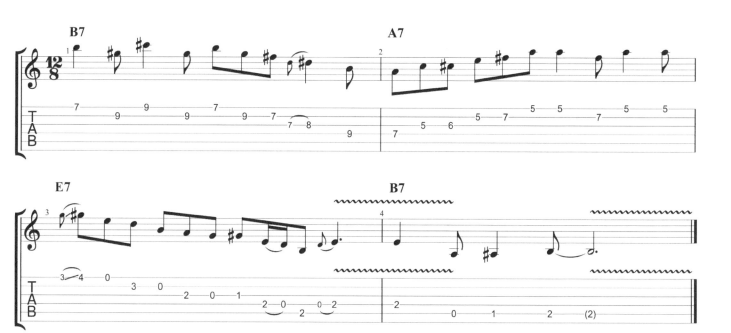

If nothing else, this approach helps you access a few new note choices (many of the notes in B Major Pentatonic don't exist in E Major or Minor Pentatonic) and gives you more soloing options.

Check out Stevie Ray Vaughan's excellent *Honey Bee* from *Couldn't Stand the Weather* to hear this approach in action in the intro to the tune. You'll often hear this major pentatonic approach used in the turnaround section of a blues, which is what we're going to study next.

Chapter Nine – Turnarounds and Outros

A turnaround is an important, if slightly clichéd type of blues lick that normally begins in the eleventh bar of the 12-bar blues. Often it will start on the second beat of the bar and approach the dominant chord in bar twelve in a stepwise movement.

Every blues guitarist has their favourite turnarounds and will play many variations of the same basic structure, but these licks will all have an internal strength and logic that the listener can follow as the melody pulls the final bars of the tune back to the beginning. The lick literally "turns the song around".

The best way to understand how a turnaround works, along with its placement and feel is to learn a few turnaround licks. The following examples are all played over the final four chords of a 12-bar blues in E. I'll play a simple lick over the first two bars, then play a simple turnaround lick that leads into the final B7 chord.

We'll start with some simple ideas that gradually get a bit more involved. Notice how all of the lines lead smoothly to the notes of the B7 chord.

Example 9a

Example 9b

Example 9c

Example 9d

The amazing thing about turnarounds is that not only do they work beautifully to turn a tune around, they can also serve as the *intro* to a tune. By changing a couple of notes, the same lick will work well in both contexts. In fact, most blues tunes end with an altered turnaround like this.

In the previous examples, the melody led strongly to notes in the dominant B7 chord which made the music feel like it was going to *turn around* for another chorus. If we play exactly the same thing but change those final notes so that the line leads to the *tonic* (home) E7 chord, then it will always bring the tune nicely to a finish.

The following examples show how the turnarounds above can be converted into outro/ending phrases.

Example 9e

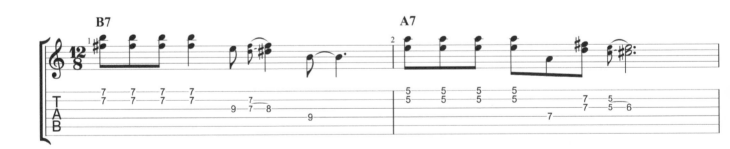

Example 9f

Example 9g

Example 9h

It's amazing how altering just a couple of notes can change the whole emphasis of the lick.

Here are some blues turnaround licks that work in the key of A. They target the dominant E7 chord in bar twelve. Again, they begin with a lick played over bars nine and ten before the turnaround starts in bar eleven.

Example 9i

Example 9j

Finally, here are the same turnaround licks played as outros. The final few notes are altered to target the home A7 chord instead of the E7.

Example 9k

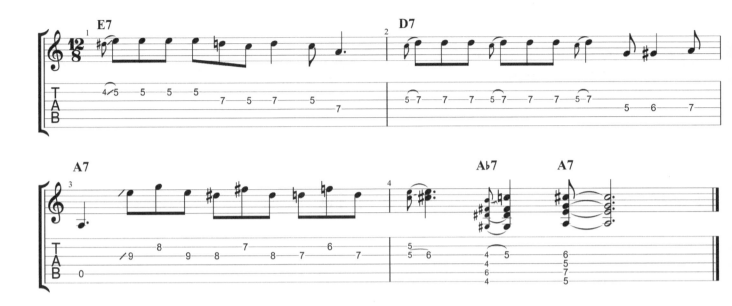

Example 9l

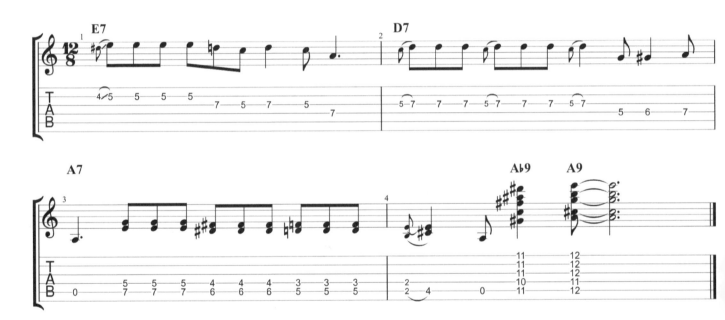

Now it's over to you. Put on a blues backing track and improvise a solo freely over the first ten bars before playing a turnaround lick in bar eleven. Don't worry if it takes you a few goes to get the placement right – there are a lot of things you have to balance here. Not only do you have to think about the solo you're creating, you need to feel exactly where you are in the blues progression. Listening to a lot of Chicago blues guitar music will help as there's almost always a strong turnaround in each chorus. Jam along and try to play your turnaround at the same time.

Your job now is to collect as many turnaround licks as you can! Try to figure out the ones you like and add them to your vocabulary.

Chapter Ten – Question and Answer Phrasing

If there's one thing I hope you've learned so far, it's that blues soloing doesn't just consist of noodling around a pentatonic scale. It's obviously important to convey emotion through your playing, but another piece of that jigsaw is how to structure the journey you will take your audience on.

If you simply play an endless stream of notes with no breaks, you'll quickly lose your audience's attention, but if you "talk" in sentences they understand, they'll stay with you and engage more in what you're saying on the instrument.

The best (and most authentic) way to help your audience follow you is to use *question and answer* phrasing.

Blues music isn't just about guitar solos. Far from it. In fact, if you're reading this book as a guitarist there's a good chance that you're looking to play isolated, self-contained solos, on your own or in front of a band. While that's a worthy pursuit, it's only half the story. If you go and listen to any live blues band there is almost always a singer, and if you listen to the singer, you'll quickly start to understand how the blues is phrased.

More often than not the singer will sing a short lyric (the "question") before a second instrument, such as a guitar, trumpet or piano will play an answering phrase in the gap before the next line. This is the essence of question and answer phrasing. Copying this structure in your solos helps the audience follow the music.

However, when you're practising at home you might not have a handy singer to work with, so you need to pretend to be one with your guitar.

When you're soloing, think in terms of *pairs* of phrases, not just the next lick you're going to play. The first phrase is the "question". This should create a little bit of musical tension by ending on an unresolved note. The next phrase is the "answer", which will normally, but not always resolve the question.

I don't want to go off on a massive theory tangent, so rather than discussing the theory behind which notes will create tension at which points in the chord sequence, it's best that you learn this skill by copying some good examples of question and answer phrasing. As soon as you begin to hear it in action, you'll naturally start to find the right notes to play.

The following example is two choruses of a blues in E. Think of it as being split into four-bar sections.

Each four-bar section contains either a two-bar question phrase followed by a two-bar answer, a one-bar phrase followed by a one-bar answer, or a combination of both. Listen to how the first phrase is deliberately answered by the second.

Example 10a

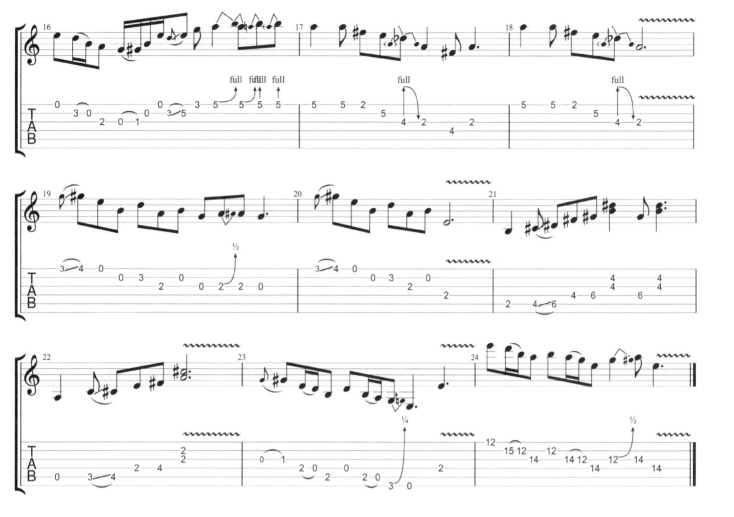

You won't always use such a rigid form in your playing, but when you're starting out this approach will help you to play in a way that resonates with your audience.

Don't forget, any phrase can start early (before the bar) or late by leaving *space* before you play.

Chapter Eleven – Example Soloing Scheme

In this book we've looked at a lot of sound options for soloing on the 12-bar blues. These include minor pentatonics, major pentatonics, and playing a different major pentatonic on each chord of the progression.

With all these options, you might be wondering which choice is best to play when. The honest answer is, you must experiment to see what *you* like the sound of! However, I do want to give you a tried and trusted soloing approach that works well for me and many of my students.

By now, you should take it as read that the major pentatonic and minor pentatonic will sound good at any point in the progression. However, the following chart shows a 12-bar blues in E and I've written my favourite sounds to use at each point in the progression above the chords. You'll see that the chord progression has an A7 chord in bar two. This "quick change" is a common little alteration that sounds great and gives you more to latch onto as a soloist.

E Major Pentatonic	E Minor Pentatonic	E Minor Pentatonic	E Major Pentatonic
E7	A7	E7	E7
E Minor Pentatonic	E Minor Pentatonic	E Major Pentatonic	E Minor Pentatonic
A7	A7	E7	E7
E Major Pentatonic	E Minor Pentatonic	E Minor Pentatonic / Turnaround	
B7	A7	E7	B7

The above chart shows a very "broad strokes" scheme. In essence it shows one really great movement – every time the chord changes from E7 to A7 I accentuate the movement by moving from E Major Pentatonic to E Minor Pentatonic. In fact, you really don't need to play E Major Pentatonic for the whole E7 bar. Simply add a few notes just before the change to A7. The E Minor Pentatonic is a great way to *articulate* this chord change and help to link your guitar solo to the harmony of the song.

The following 24-bar solo stays close to the scheme shown above. Notice where I play the major pentatonic for a whole bar, and notice when I just add a few notes towards the end of the bar before the chord changes to A7.

Example 11a

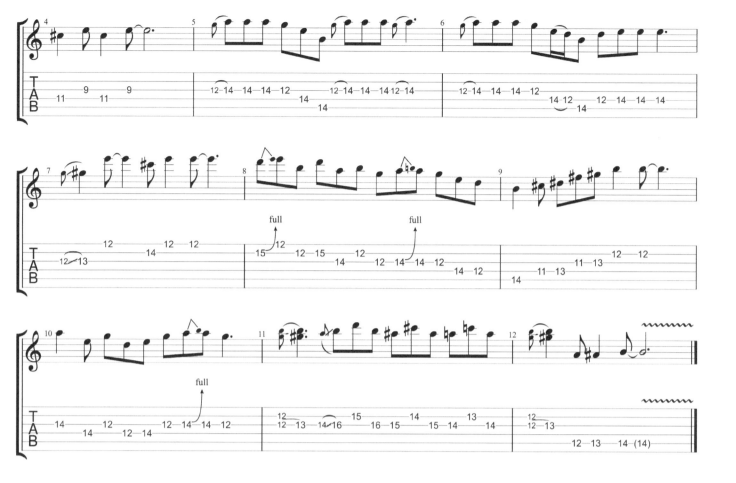

While a soloing scheme like this may feel restrictive at first, it will actually force you to become more imaginative in your own improvisation as you have to be creative within its confines. Of course, if you don't like my approach, please do change it and come up with your own structure. Remember that you can play major or minor pentatonic sounds at any point, and the better you get at combining them, as I taught you in Chapter Seven, the more fluent your solos will become.

Chapter Twelve – Conclusions and Final Solos

And there we have it, your complete guide to becoming a full-blown blues soloist. Apart from sheer practice, your best tools now are *listening* and *jamming*.

The more you listen to great musicians, the more you'll pick up and the more influences will appear in your playing. It's the same reason why great writers read all the time.

The blues isn't a solitary music, it evokes an emotion that is best shared. As soon as you're able to play some chords and explore simple solos, it's time to get out of the practice room and into a jam band. Make music with as many people as possible – ideally those who are better than you. They'll quickly bring you up to their level and playing with them will teach you more than you'll ever be able to learn on your own. I mean it, go and get playing!

I want to leave you with a couple of slightly more challenging 12-bar blues solos that you can work towards playing. The first is in the key of E, and the second is in the key of A. They'll both teach you what a well-constructed, powerful solo sounds like and they combine many of the ideas we've studied in this book.

Have fun, and good luck!

Joseph

Example 12a

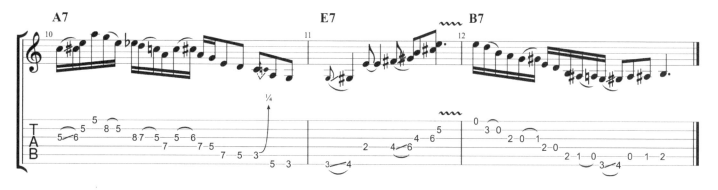

103

Example 12b

More Blues Books From Fundamental Changes

100 Classic Blues Licks for Guitar

Beyond Rhythm Guitar

Complete Guide to Playing Blues Guitar: Book 1 Rhythm Guitar

Complete Guide to Playing Blues Guitar: Book 2 Melodic Phrasing

Complete Guide to Playing Blues Guitar: Book 3 Beyond Pentatonics

Complete Guide to Playing Blues Guitar Compilation

Fingerstyle Blues Guitar

Slide Guitar Soloing Techniques

The CAGED System and 100 Licks for Blues Guitar

Guitar: Pentatonic and Blues Scales

Made in United States
Troutdale, OR
12/30/2024

27439978R20060